Understanding World History

The War in Afghanistan

Stuart A. Kallen

Bruno Leone
Series Consultant

ReferencePoint
Press®

San Diego, CA

© 2014 ReferencePoint Press, Inc.
Printed in the United States

For more information, contact:
ReferencePoint Press, Inc.
PO Box 27779
San Diego, CA 92198
www. ReferencePointPress.com

LIBRARY OF CONGRESS CATALOGING-IN-PUBLICATION DATA

Kallen, Stuart A., 1955-
   The war in Afghanistan / by Stuart A. Kallen.
      pages cm. — (Understanding world history)
   Includes bibliographical references and index.
   ISBN 13: 978-1-60152-632-8 (hardback)
   ISBN 10: 1-60152-632-6 (hardback)
   1. Afghan War, 2001- —Juvenile literature. I. Title.
   DS371.412.K35 2013
   958.104'7--dc23
                                                    2013028193

Contents

Foreword

When the Puritans first emigrated from England to America in 1630, they believed that their journey was blessed by a covenant between themselves and God. By the terms of that covenant they agreed to establish a community in the New World dedicated to what they believed was the true Christian faith. God, in turn, would reward their fidelity by making certain that they and their descendants would always experience his protection and enjoy material prosperity. Moreover, the Lord guaranteed that their land would be seen as a shining beacon—or in their words, a "city upon a hill,"—which the rest of the world would view with admiration and respect. By embracing this notion that God could and would shower his favor and special blessings upon them, the Puritans were adopting the providential philosophy of history—meaning that history is the unfolding of a plan established or guided by a higher intelligence.

The concept of intercession by a divine power is only one of many explanations of the driving forces of world history. Historians and philosophers alike have subscribed to numerous other ideas. For example, the ancient Greeks and Romans argued that history is cyclical. Nations and civilizations, according to these ancients of the Western world, rise and fall in unpredictable cycles; the only certainty is that these cycles will persist throughout an endless future. The German historian Oswald Spengler (1880–1936) echoed the ancients to some degree in his controversial study *The Decline of the West*. Spengler asserted that all civilizations inevitably pass through stages comparable to the life span of a person: childhood, youth, adulthood, old age, and, eventually, death. As the title of his work implies, Western civilization is currently entering its final stage.

Joining those who see purpose and direction in history are thinkers who completely reject the idea of meaning or certainty. Rather, they reason that since there are far too many random and unseen factors at work on the earth, historians would be unwise to endorse historical predictability of any type. Warfare (both nuclear and conventional), plagues, earthquakes, tsunamis, meteor showers, and other catastrophic world-changing events have loomed large throughout history and prehistory. In his essay "A Free Man's Worship," philosopher and mathematician Bertrand Russell (1872–1970) supported this argument, which many refer to as the nihilist or chaos theory of history. According to Russell, history follows no preordained path. Rather, the earth itself and all life on earth resulted from, as Russell describes it, an "accidental collocation of atoms." Based on this premise, he pessimistically concluded that all human achievement will eventually be "buried beneath the debris of a universe in ruins."

Whether history does or does not have an underlying purpose, historians, journalists, and countless others have nonetheless left behind a record of human activity tracing back nearly 6,000 years. From the dawn of the great ancient Near Eastern civilizations of Mesopotamia and Egypt to the modern economic and military behemoths China and the United States, humanity's deeds and misdeeds have been and continue to be monitored and recorded. The distinguished British scholar Arnold Toynbee (1889–1975), in his widely acclaimed twelve-volume work entitled *A Study of History,* studied twenty-one different civilizations that have passed through history's pages. He noted with certainty that others would follow.

In the final analysis, the academic and journalistic worlds mostly regard history as a record and explanation of past events. From a more practical perspective, history represents a sequence of building blocks—cultural, technological, military, and political—ready to be utilized and enhanced or maligned and perverted by the present. What that means is that all societies—whether advanced civilizations or preliterate tribal cultures—leave a legacy for succeeding generations to either embrace or disregard.

Recognizing the richness and fullness of history, the ReferencePoint Press Understanding World History series fosters an evaluation and interpretation of history and its influence on later generations. Each volume in the series approaches its subject chronologically and topically, with specific focus on nations, periods, or pivotal events. Primary and secondary source quotations are included, along with complete source notes and suggestions for further research.

Moreover, the series reflects the truism that the key to understanding the present frequently lies in the past. With that in mind, each series title concludes with a legacy chapter that highlights the bonds between past and present and, more important, demonstrates that world history is a continuum of peoples and ideas, sometimes hidden but there nonetheless, waiting to be discovered by those who choose to look.

Important Events of the War in Afghanistan

2001
On September 11 al Qaeda terrorists hijack four commercial jetliners and fly two of them into the World Trade Center in New York City and one into the Pentagon in Washington, DC. The fourth plane crashes in Pennsylvania. The attack kills 2,977 victims, plus all 19 hijackers. On October 7 the United States launches Operation Enduring Freedom, invading Afghanistan to overthrow the Taliban government and wipe out al Qaeda.

2003
On March 19 the United States launches Operation Iraqi Freedom, invading Iraq with 148,000 American troops.

2002   **2004**   **2006**

2002
On April 17 Americans learn for the first time that terrorist mastermind Osama bin Laden escaped from Afghanistan and safely made his way to Pakistan the previous December.

2006
In January the United Nations International Security Assistance Force takes over military operations in southern Afghanistan as the United States diverts its military resources to Iraq.

2004
In October Hamid Karzai is elected president in Afghanistan's first democratic election.

2005
Taliban leader Mullah Omar divides Afghanistan into five war zones and launches a renewed insurgency against US-led forces, with a dramatic increase in ambushes, suicide bombings, and attacks with improvised explosive devices.

2009
In November Obama announces an additional thirty thousand American soldiers will be sent to Afghanistan as part of a troop surge meant to bring the total number of coalition forces to one hundred thousand.

2007
Between March and May fifty-five hundred coalition troops conduct the largest multinational action of the war, Operation Achilles, in Helmand Province.

2011
On May 1 US Navy SEAL commandos assault Bin Laden's compound in Abbottabad, Pakistan, killing the terrorist leader with a bullet to the head.

2013
As of June 2,245 American troops have been killed in the war in Afghanistan.

2008   **2010**   **2012**   **2014**

2008
On November 4 Barack Obama is elected president of the United States after promising to end the war in Iraq and win the war in Afghanistan.

2012
The United States reaches an agreement with the Afghan government to withdraw all American combat troops by the end of 2014.

2010
In July the website WikiLeaks publishes more than ninety-one thousand classified US military reports with intelligence about drone strikes, civilian deaths, Taliban attacks, and other top secret information about the war in Afghanistan.

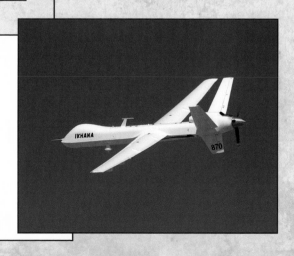

The Defining Characteristics of the War in Afghanistan

October 7, 2012, marked the eleventh anniversary of the US war in Afghanistan. Several days later news columnist Arianna Huffington wrote, "In addition to being America's longest war, Afghanistan is a contender for being America's least-talked-about war."[1] In one short sentence, Huffington summed up two crucial aspects about the war in Afghanistan. It lasted more than twelve years, and during most of that time the attention of the media and the American public was elsewhere. Afghanistan was rarely discussed during the numerous presidential debates leading up to the November 2012 election. Perhaps the lack of interest could be traced to negative feelings about the war. In 2012 only 30 percent of Americans thought the war was worth fighting, whereas 70 percent wanted the US military to leave Afghanistan as quickly as possible.

This was not the case when the war began on October 7, 2001, and more than eight in ten Americans supported the cause. The invasion of Afghanistan began less than one month after the 9/11 terrorist attacks that brought down the World Trade Center's Twin Towers in New York City and severely damaged the Pentagon in Washington, DC. The Afghan war, known as Operation Enduring Freedom, was launched to destroy the terrorist group al Qaeda and its leader Osama bin Laden, the mastermind behind 9/11. Al Qaeda had numerous training camps in Afghanistan, a nation led by the Taliban government, an Islamic fundamentalist regime.

The Afghan war was conducted by the International Security Assistance Force (ISAF), established by the United Nations Security Council in December 2001. Widely referred to as the coalition, the ISAF consisted of more than fifty countries and was led by the United States, which contributed about three-quarters of the troops.

In the beginning, the war went very well. By November 2001 US Special Forces, aided by massive airpower, had defeated the Taliban and sent al Qaeda and its allies fleeing over the border to Pakistan. In October 2002, on the first anniversary of the war, Defense Secretary Donald Rumsfeld announced, "The Taliban are gone. The al Qaeda are gone."[2]

The Forgotten War

Less than six months after Rumsfeld's statement, the United States invaded Iraq. President George W. Bush launched Operation Iraqi Freedom on the mistaken premise that Iraq's brutal dictator, Saddam Hussein, was building weapons of mass destruction. With the launch of Operation Iraqi Freedom, personnel, money, and supplies were diverted from Afghanistan to Iraq. By the end of 2003, there were about eighteen thousand American troops in Afghanistan, aided by about forty-five hundred coalition troops. Meanwhile, sixty-seven thousand US soldiers were fighting in Iraq, a country nearly twice the size of Afghanistan but with an equal number of people, around 30 million.

By 2005 the media and the American public were focused on the much larger war in Iraq, which was going badly. The media began to refer to the war in Afghanistan as the "Other War" and the "Forgotten War." Although one thousand US servicemen and servicewomen had lost their lives in the Afghan war by this time, major media outlets almost stopped covering the war. In 2001 the three nightly network newscasts aired a total of 1,288 minutes on the war in Afghanistan. In all of 2005 they aired 147 minutes. Only 13 minutes were devoted to the hunt for the world's most wanted terrorist, Bin Laden.

A Resurgent Enemy

Even as Afghanistan faded from public view, the war was entering a second phase. The Taliban staged a resurgence, operating from small, mobile camps established along the Pakistan border. The Taliban hardly ever numbered more than several thousand fighters at a time. However, working in groups of around fifty, they coordinated attacks on isolated American military outposts and convoys of soldiers, as well as Afghan police and military units.

US forces were often attacked indirectly, through rocket strikes on bases and homemade bombs called improvised explosive devices (IEDs), which were placed along roadsides. The bombs, which cost less than thirty dollars each, were made from used artillery shells filled with plastic or fertilizer-based explosives. The IEDs were detonated remotely by specially adapted cell phones.

Targeted by insurgents, US Marines run for cover in Afghanistan. An international coalition, led by the United States, invaded Afghanistan to destroy the terrorist group al Qaeda and the Taliban government that supported its activities.

IEDs were the main weapon of the enemy insurgents. Difficult to detect and horrific when detonated, IEDs were responsible for two out of three coalition deaths during the Afghan war. Many thousands more were grievously wounded by IEDs. The crude IEDs and small arms of the enemy were pitted against the most sophisticated weapons on earth. The United States used high-tech gunships, special navigation gear, radar, and other electronics to find and destroy the enemy. Super "cave-buster" bombs were used to penetrate mountain hideouts where al Qaeda and Taliban soldiers were hiding.

The Longest War

In November 2008 Barack Obama was elected president of the United States, inheriting two wars launched by his predecessor, George W. Bush. The Afghan war was seven years old and showed no sign of winding down. After nearly a year of debate with American military leaders, Obama announced a new strategy called the "troop surge" in November 2009. By this time the number of soldiers in Afghanistan had gradually increased to sixty-eight thousand. The surge added an additional thirty-three thousand US troops by mid-2010. The rapid deployment was meant to break the Taliban's momentum and turn the war around.

On July 7, 2010, seven months into the surge, the war in Afghanistan became the longest continuous war in US history. Another historical landmark was achieved on May 1, 2011, when Bin Laden was shot and killed by US Special Forces in his hideout in Abbottabad, Pakistan.

The Death Toll Climbs

One month after Bin Laden's death, Obama announced the beginning of a gradual withdrawal from Afghanistan. However, the situation in the country remained uncertain, according to a statement by US vice president Joe Biden: "Currently there is little capacity for the Afghan government to execute many of the functions of government. In many areas of the country, local officials have close to no knowledge of how to govern or even basic knowledge of payroll or budget. . . . The idea of a strong rule of law under a centralized . . . government is not realistic."[3]

Despite Biden's assessment, in early 2012 the United States reached an agreement with the Afghan government to withdraw all combat troops by the end of 2014. Throughout that period, coalition soldiers continued to die from IEDs, suicide bombings, and other attacks. As of July 2013 there were more than 3,354 coalition deaths in Afghanistan. Of those, 2,255 were US troops.

Even after the United States began reducing the number of combat troops, the US Department of Defense announced that the United States would keep ten thousand to twenty thousand soldiers in Afghanistan, possibly until 2024. These soldiers would provide protection to government officials and train military and police forces at a cost of $4 billion annually.

While the United States continued to invest in Afghanistan, the Afghan government remained extremely corrupt. Paying bribes to officials, police, and other government workers was part of daily life. In 2012 more than half of all Afghans polled said they paid bribes when requesting public services. According to a study by the United Nations Office on Drugs and Crime, the cost of those bribes was estimated at $3.9 billion. Meanwhile, the Taliban continued to exert great power. In 2013 the insurgents doubled the number of attacks on civilians, soldiers, and government officials from the previous year. This made 2013 one of the most violent years of the war.

When the United States went to war in Afghanistan, the goal was to kill Bin Laden and destroy the government that provided sanctuary to al Qaeda. Most Americans assumed the mission would be accomplished within a few years, if not sooner. However, after twelve years, billions of US dollars spent, and thousands of coalition deaths, the situation for average Afghans was little better. Before and after the war, Afghanistan was one of the world's poorest countries, with an incompetent government, a ruined infrastructure, and millions of people living on the edge of starvation. Whatever the fate of the Taliban and its opponents, the struggles of the Afghan people will undoubtedly persist for years to come.

Chapter 1

What Events Led to the War in Afghanistan?

September 11, 2001, began as a beautiful, clear blue morning in New York City. The day turned into one of shock and horror at 8:46 a.m. when hijackers flew a Boeing 757 jet into the north tower of the 110-story Twin Towers of the World Trade Center (WTC). Seventeen minutes later another Boeing jetliner hit the south tower. At 9:37, hijackers crashed a jet into the Pentagon in Washington, DC. Less than a half hour later, a fourth hijacked jetliner was flown into the ground in Shanksville, Pennsylvania, after passengers fought for control of the plane. This plane was likely headed for the US Capitol or the White House. By 10:28 both towers of the World Trade Center had collapsed. The final death toll of the 9/11 terrorist attack was 2,977, not including all 19 hijackers who died while conducting the attack.

Minutes after the second jet smashed into the Twin Towers, CIA director George Tenet was at an emergency meeting filled with intelligence, military, and national security personnel. Tenet said later, "I don't think there was a person in the room who had the least doubt that we were in the middle of a full-scale assault orchestrated by al Qaeda. . . . The whole operation looked, smelled, and tasted like bin Laden."[4]

Immediately after the attacks, the FBI initiated the largest criminal investigation in American history. Code-named PENTTBOM (Pentagon/Twin Towers Bombing), it involved more than seven thousand of the bureau's eleven thousand special agents. Within days the

FBI had identified the nineteen hijackers through flight logs, credit card records, and other information. As Tenet initially suspected, all nineteen men were connected to the terrorist organization al Qaeda, and they were carrying out orders given by Osama bin Laden.

"Bin Laden Determined to Strike"

At the time of the attacks, most Americans knew little about al Qaeda or Bin Laden. However, Bin Laden was well-known to security expert Richard A. Clarke and other highly placed government officials. Clarke had been appointed national coordinator for security, infrastructure protection, and counter-terrorism in 1998 by President Bill Clinton. He stayed at his post after George W. Bush became president in January 2001 and met with administration security officials within days. At this meeting, Clarke warned, "Al Qaeda is at war with us, it is a highly capable organization, probably with sleeper cells in the U.S., and it is clearly planning a major series of attacks against us; we must act decisively and quickly."[5] Clarke's fears were heightened months later when an August CIA briefing for the president displayed the headline "Bin Laden Determined to Strike in U.S."[6]

Clarke could not state exactly when or where an attack might occur, and his warnings went unheeded by Bush administration officials. However, al Qaeda had long been advocating violence against the United States. And long before 9/11 Bin Laden had been laying the groundwork for events that would one day lead to the war in Afghanistan.

Waging War Against America

Bin Laden was born in 1957 to one of the wealthiest families in the oil-rich kingdom of Saudi Arabia. His father, who had twenty-four wives and an estimated fifty-seven children, had made a fortune building highways and palaces for the Saudi royal family. As a teen, Bin Laden became a devout Sunni Muslim and an adherent of sharia, the strict Islamic laws and customs developed in the eighth and ninth centuries.

In 1988 Bin Laden formed al Qaeda, which translates from Arabic as "the base." He used his family's vast wealth to operate al Qaeda as a

Black smoke and flames engulf the Twin Towers of New York's World Trade Center after both were hit by hijacked commercial airliners on September 11, 2001. The terrorist attack, which also involved two other hijacked airliners, led to the US war in Afghanistan.

multinational, stateless army. The organization was dedicated to waging a global jihad, or religious battle, against those who did not believe in Islamic fundamentalist ideals. Bin Laden moved al Qaeda's operations to Afghanistan in 1996 after the Taliban took over the country under the rule of Mullah Omar.

Upon gaining power, the Taliban initiated a harsh interpretation of sharia law. The government banned dancing, television, photography, soccer, playing or listening to music, and even kite flying. Afghan women were required to cover themselves from head to toe, were not allowed to leave home without being accompanied by a male relative, and were prohibited from working or attending school. Anyone who violated the strict rules could be stoned to death, publicly executed, or subjected to amputation of the hands. The Taliban regime burned all books except for the Koran, the holy book of Islam, and destroyed ancient non-Islamic artworks and statues. The Taliban even banned what they termed British and American hairstyles. Bin Laden described Taliban-controlled Afghanistan as the only truly Islamic country in the Muslim world.

In 1998 Bin Laden issued a fatwa, or binding religious edict, that declared war against the United States and its allies: "The ruling to kill the Americans and their allies—civilians and military—is an individual duty for every Muslim who can do it in any country in which it is possible to do it."[7]

Bin Laden was angered by the presence of US troops in Saudi Arabia. American soldiers had been there since 1990, protecting oil shipments through the Persian Gulf and enforcing economic sanctions against Iraq. Bin Laden believed the presence of American troops in the holy Islamic cities of Mecca and Medina profaned the sacred soil. As Bin Laden told an interviewer in 1998, "The call to wage war against America was made because America has spear-headed the crusade against the Islamic nation, sending tens of thousands of its troops to the land of the two Holy Mosques over and above its meddling in its affairs and its politics, and its support of the oppressive, corrupt and tyrannical regime that is in control [of Saudi Arabia]."[8]

Orchestrating al Qaeda Attacks

Bin Laden saw an opportunity for his cause in Afghanistan. He offered the Taliban money, soldiers, and military training; in return they welcomed him and his organization into their country. In the years that followed, Bin Laden used his base in Afghanistan to orchestrate several al Qaeda attacks on US interests. In August 1998 al Qaeda simultaneously bombed two US embassies, one in Dar es Salaam, Tanzania, the other in Nairobi, Kenya. In the two incidents more than three hundred civilians were killed and nearly four thousand wounded, most of them locals. Several weeks later the United States retaliated by launching eighty Tomahawk cruise missiles at al Qaeda training camps in Afghanistan. The following November Bin Laden was indicted in US federal court for his role in the embassy bombings.

Another terrorist attack occurred in October 2000 when a group of al Qaeda fighters bombed the US Navy missile destroyer USS *Cole* while it was refueling in a harbor in Yemen. The suicide attack killed seventeen American navy personnel and injured thirty-nine.

These attacks were still fresh in the minds of national security officials in the United States on September 11, 2001. Within days of the 9/11 attack, however, Bin Laden released a statement denying personal involvement but supporting the actions of the hijackers: "I would like to assure the world that I did not plan the recent attacks, which seems to have been planned by people for personal reasons. I have been living in the Islamic emirate of Afghanistan and following its leaders' rules. The current leader does not allow me to exercise such operations."[9] (Bin Laden finally admitted his involvement in 9/11 in a videotaped message recorded on October 30, 2004.)

In Afghanistan the Taliban's foreign minister, Wakil Ahmed Muttawakil, denounced the 9/11 attacks and denied any connection to his government. More than one thousand Afghan clerics signed a letter expressing sadness for the civilian deaths caused by the hijackers.

Bin Laden Wanted Dead or Alive

Even as Bin Laden and the Taliban were issuing denials, the US government was taking decisive steps toward stopping al Qaeda. On September 12, 2001, the US Department of State began assembling a global coalition of nations. According to national security adviser Condoleezza Rice, "It was Secretary Rumsfeld who came up with the notion that . . . there would be members of the coalition who would not want to participate in military activity, but who might have exactly the right piece of information through intelligence sources that [would prove] very important in bringing down Al Qaeda."[10] The coalition was quickly joined by the United Kingdom, Germany, and France, and these three nations offered to add combat troops, money, and military equipment to the fight against the terrorists.

On September 14 Congress gave the president permission to go to war, passing a resolution called the Authorization for Use of Military Force Against Terrorists (AUMF). The AUMF authorized the president to "use all necessary and appropriate force against those nations, organizations, or persons he determines planned, authorized, committed, or aided the terrorist attacks . . . or harbored such organizations or persons."[11]

The US Constitution states that only Congress can declare war, and the wording of the AUMF was not a formal declaration of war against Afghanistan. Instead, it granted the president the freedom to wage war

The United States government offered a $25 million reward for the capture of Osama bin Laden (pictured), the man who orchestrated the 9/11 attacks. President George W. Bush also demanded that Afghan's Taliban government turn over al Qaeda leaders and close terrorist training camps.

against any person or group—anywhere—who he believed was guilty of planning or committing terrorist acts against the United States. Never before in American history had any president been given such broad powers. However, with the fires still burning at Ground Zero where the Twin Towers had once stood, the AUMF was approved by every senator. Only one member of Congress, Representative Barbara Lee from California, voted against the resolution. Lee wrote at the time:

> It was a blank check to the president to attack anyone involved in the Sept. 11 events—anywhere, in any country, without regard to our nation's long-term foreign policy, economic and national security interests, and without time limit. In granting these overly broad powers, the Congress failed its responsibility to understand the dimensions of its declaration. I could not support such a grant of war-making authority to the president.[12]

Most Americans were eager for revenge after 9/11 and, according to polls taken at the time, the president essentially had the nation's full support. On September 20 Bush gave a televised speech to the nation, seen by 80 million Americans. He blamed the Taliban for providing a safe haven to Bin Laden. He demanded that the regime turn over al Qaeda's leaders to the United States and shut down the terrorist training camps. Mullah Omar refused Bush's demands. This prompted the United States to offer a $10 million reward for Omar's capture, along with a $25 million reward for Bin Laden. Several days later Vice President Dick Cheney said he wanted Bin Laden's "head on a platter," and Bush said, "I want justice and there's an old poster out West that says, 'Dead or Alive.'"[13]

Organizing an Antiwar Movement

The tough talk from the president and vice president alarmed some who did not think the 9/11 attacks warranted invasion of Afghanistan. Critics noted that none of the perpetrators were from Afghanistan. Fifteen of the nineteen hijackers, along with Bin Laden, were from Saudi Arabia. The rest were from Egypt, the United Arab Emirates, and Lebanon.

In response to the march toward war, a worldwide antiwar movement was organized. It was led by a group called the ANSWER Coalition (*ANSWER* stands for "Act Now to Stop War and End Racism").

ANSWER was formed on September 14, 2001, and its first demonstrations were held on September 29. About twenty-five thousand people marched in Washington, DC, while fifteen thousand demonstrated in San Francisco. Smaller demonstrations took place in Los Angeles, New York City, Chicago, Boston, and elsewhere. During the next several weeks, international protests attracted crowds of ten thousand or more in Spain, Netherlands, the United Kingdom, Sweden, Germany, Italy, and Australia.

Fighting in Rugged Terrain

While those opposed to a US invasion of Afghanistan protested, the State Department assembled a global coalition of nations willing to help the United States fight a war in Afghanistan. Britain, Canada, Germany, and Australia offered to contribute soldiers, aircraft, and logistical support. France, Italy, and Japan promised aircraft carriers, military engineering teams, transport aircraft, and refueling ships. Eventually, the coalition was joined by fifty nations, including El Salvador, Mongolia, and Estonia. However, the main fighting force was made up of American and British soldiers.

In preparation for the invasion, the CIA and the US military drew up plans for a war tailored to the situation in Afghanistan. The landlocked country, which is slightly smaller than Texas, is one of the poorest and least developed in the world. The nation is dominated by the Hindu Kush mountain range, which rises to 24,500 feet (7,468 m) and covers all but the north-central and southwest portions of the country.

Afghanistan's extreme, rugged topography and lack of good roads would make it difficult for ground troops to maneuver. This was the case when the Afghans fought the Soviet Union from 1979 to 1989. The Soviets had engaged in traditional warfare, using soldiers to hold on to major cities while deploying tens of thousands of troops to the countryside to fight the Islamic tribal leaders known as the mujahideen. Local Afghans, accustomed to the terrain, easily outmaneuvered the heavily burdened foreign soldiers.

President Bush Speaks to the Nation

On September 20, 2001, President George W. Bush gave a televised speech to a nation still in shock from the terrorist attacks of September 11. More than 80 million Americans watched the president as he linked the Taliban to Osama bin Laden and al Qaeda:

> By aiding and abetting murder, the Taliban regime is committing murder. And tonight the United States of America makes the following demands on the Taliban: Deliver to United States authorities all of the leaders of Al Qaeda who hide in your land. Release all foreign nationals, including American citizens you have unjustly imprisoned. Protect foreign journalists, diplomats and aid workers in your country. Close immediately and permanently every terrorist training camp in Afghanistan. And hand over every terrorist and every person and their support structure to appropriate authorities. Give the United States full access to terrorist training camps, so we can make sure they are no longer operating. These demands are not open to negotiation or discussion. The Taliban must act and act immediately. . . . [We] will pursue nations that provide aid or safe haven to terrorism. Every nation in every region now has a decision to make: Either you are with us or you are with the terrorists.

George Bush, "Transcript of President Bush's Address," CNN, September 21, 2001. http://archives.cnn.com.

Unconventional War

The Afghans eventually sent the Soviets home in defeat. However, during the decade of war, Soviet bombers destroyed much of the country's buildings, roads, railroads, power lines, and other facilities. After the

Map labels: UZBEKISTAN, TAJIKISTAN, TURKMENISTAN, Mazar-e Sharif, Hindu Kush Mountains, N, Kabul, AFGHANISTAN, Jalalabad, HELMAND PROVINCE, Kandahar, IRAN, PAKISTAN

Soviets left, a civil war raged from 1992 to 1996, destroying most of what was left of Afghanistan's infrastructure. As Rumsfeld commented on September 30, 2001:

> You're dealing with a country that doesn't have high-value targets, that doesn't have armies, navies and air forces, its capital [Kabul] has been pummeled by the Soviet Union to the point that it's rubble and by internal fighting among everybody there—there's not much that [the terrorists] hold dear. They live in caves, they live in tents, they move constantly. And what we have to do is to deal with that kind of an enemy in a way that's appropriate.[14]

Military planners developed an unconventional warfare strategy. Rather than sending in tens of thousands of ground troops, small teams of CIA paramilitary fighters and US Special Operations Forces (called special ops or SOF) prepared to link up with Afghan resistance fighters known as the Northern Alliance. Special operations forces consist of highly trained soldiers from all branches of the US military. The Northern Alliance forces consisted of anti-Taliban mujahideen who exercised military and political control over armed tribal factions in rural Afghanistan. The Northern Alliance was assembled from Afghan leaders who were ousted in 1996 when the Taliban came to power. Officially known as the United Islamic Front for the Salvation of Afghanistan, the Northern Alliance was the strongest armed group of fighters in Afghanistan in 2001.

The American strategy involved arming, funding, and fighting alongside the Northern Alliance. Bush explained the strategy this way: "By mating up our forces with the local opposition, we would avoid looking like a conqueror or occupier. America would help the Afghan people liberate themselves."[15]

Four Phases

By the third week in September, the CIA was moving its first teams into countries to the north of Afghanistan. These included Uzbekistan, Kyrgyzstan, and Tajikistan. US general Tommy Franks was named commander of the impending war, which was code-named Operation Enduring Freedom.

Franks presented a four-phase plan to Bush. Phase I would move US fighters into Afghanistan to link up with the Northern Alliance. American airdrops would provide arms, food, and medicine to local ground forces. Phase II would see combat operations with the CIA and special operations forces calling in precision US airstrikes against Taliban and al Qaeda factions. Phase III involved operations to oust the Taliban and eliminate al Qaeda. This phase called for twelve thousand ground troops. During Phase IV, US troops and advisers would help the Afghan people build a free and functioning society.

In preparation for the war, the US Navy sent several carrier strike groups to the Persian Gulf west of Afghanistan and to the Indian Ocean south of Afghanistan. Each carrier strike group consisted of warships that included an aircraft carrier, cruisers, destroyers, and a carrier air

The Taliban

Most people in Afghanistan are members of the Pashtun culture, which revolves around a pre-Islamic code of honor called Pashtunwali. The code emphasizes honor, hospitality, protection of women, and revenge. In the Pashtun language, called Pashto, the word *Taliban* means male "students" or "seekers" of Islam. Most of the Taliban, who governed Afghanistan from 1996 to 2001, were recruited from religious schools call madrassas located in the border region between Afghanistan and Pakistan. The schools were funded by Islamic fundamentalists in Saudi Arabia and other oil-rich Persian Gulf states.

When the Taliban ruled Afghanistan, it enforced a harsh interpretation of Sunni Islam, including requirements that men grow beards and women wear full-body cloaks called burkas. Shaista Wahab, an Afghan native and professor at the University of Nebraska, describes the Taliban:

> [The Taliban] were mostly ignorant of Islamic history, law, and scholarship. The curriculum of the madrassas was based on repetition of the Qur'an [Koran] and a handful of other texts and [taught] the simple messianic, puritan values of an imagined primitive Islam. The mullahs [religious teachers and clergy] who ran the schools often confused Pashtun custom with Islamic law, especially in matters of gender roles. The young, inexperienced rank and file Taliban, many of whom had been raised on foreign handouts in refugee camps, bore little resemblance to veteran mujahedeen who were often family men with land or trades who had grown up steeped in their local social, ethnic, and religious traditions.

Shaista Wahab, *A Brief History of Afghanistan*. New York: Infobase, 2007, pp. 205–206.

wing. Each carrier air wing contained up to seventy aircraft, including fighter jets and helicopters. The USS *Kittyhawk* would serve as a base for special forces helicopters.

Team Jawbreaker

With the massive might of the US military assembling in the oceans, the CIA had placed only seven men on the ground in Afghanistan. They belonged to a group code-named Team Jawbreaker. Members of the team flew into Afghanistan in a small helicopter over the towering Hindu Kush to the Panjshir Valley on September 26. The Americans carried $3 million in cash to buy the cooperation of the Northern Alliance.

Team Jawbreaker built a small base of operations and established secure communications with the CIA Counterterrorism Center (CTC) in Washington, DC. CIA officer Gary Berntsen, leader of Team Jawbreaker, describes the mission:

> Working alongside the Afghans, the team would produce intelligence on enemy positions and capabilities that CTC headquarters would use to drive and coordinate the war. CTC would be the point of interface with the U.S. Armed Forces Central Command (CENTCOM) and General Franks' staff as they, first, managed the air campaign and, then, moved U.S. military forces into theater to eventually assume a larger role on the ground.[16]

In the days that followed, the Jawbreaker team grew to thirteen. Its members were working sixteen to twenty hours a day visiting Northern Alliance warlords in northeastern Afghanistan and making plans for the invasion. Back in the United States, the National Security Council, the CIA, and CENTCOM planned an air campaign to aid the Northern Alliance and destroy the Taliban.

Preparations for the war in Afghanistan were finished less than a month after 9/11. Most Americans assumed victory would come quickly and the war would be short and decisive. But when Rumsfeld was asked by reporters how long it would take to free Afghanistan of terrorists, he replied, "It will take years I suspect."[17]

Chapter 2

Operation Enduring Freedom

On Sunday evening, October 7, 2001, President George W. Bush addressed the American people in a somber television broadcast: "On my orders, the United States military has begun strikes against Al Qaeda terrorist training camps and military installations of the Taliban regime in Afghanistan. These carefully targeted actions are designed to disrupt the use of Afghanistan as a terrorist base of operations and to attack the military capability of the Taliban regime."[18]

As the wreckage of the World Trade Center still smoldered at Ground Zero, Operation Enduring Freedom was under way. The US Air Force dropped bombs on power stations, airports, radar facilities, and government command centers in Kabul, Kandahar, Jalalabad, and other Afghan cities. The US Navy launched about fifty long-range Tomahawk cruise missiles from ships in the Persian Gulf and Indian Ocean. Apache helicopters flown by the 101st Army Combat Aviation Brigade wiped out al Qaeda training sites.

The Taliban had few air defenses capable of resisting the US military. Most of their weapons, such as antiaircraft artillery and surface-to-air missiles, were left over from the Soviet invasion. They were outdated and of little use. By the end of the first week, coalition forces had taken total control of Afghan airspace. More than fifteen hundred bombs had been dropped, demolishing tanks and training facilities and destroying the ability of Taliban leaders to communicate with one another.

Task Force Dagger

On October 19 a group of US Special Forces teams, known as Task Force Dagger, entered Afghanistan from bases in neighboring Uzbekistan. Dagger included aviators from the 160th Special Operations Aviation Regiment and Special Tactics personnel from the Air Force Special Operations Command. Dagger's mission was to ensure the cooperation of the three most powerful Northern Alliance leaders: Abdur Rashid Dostum, Mullah Daoud, and Fahim Khan. However, the three mujahideen had often fought one another. This created a delicate situation for military planners, who needed to obtain their support. Richard W. Stewart, who served in Afghanistan as a historian for Task Force Dagger, explains:

> For political purposes, the Special Forces teams were divided among the various faction warlords as equally as possible, since the United States did not want to give the impression of favoring one of these long-term rivals, now temporary allies, over the other. . . . Afghanistan's inherent tribalism and factional splits could never be ignored despite the common enemy [the Taliban].[19]

The coalition had to act quickly to enlist the help of the mujahideen in order to establish US operating bases in northern Afghanistan. Winter was coming, and massive snowstorms would make roads over mountain passes impossible to traverse. The harsh winds and cold temperatures would make helicopter air support missions difficult and dangerous.

Close Air Support

Task Force Dagger launched its first mission on October 19, flying a twelve-person team by helicopter into Afghanistan's fourth-largest city, Mazar-i-Sharif. The city of around 375,000 was a Taliban stronghold, but the surrounding region was controlled by Dostum. According to

Two Afghan men watch as US forces bomb targets in the distance. At the beginning of the war, US forces bombed power stations, airports, radar facilities, and command centers to disable the Taliban government.

Stewart, "Dostum was an old regional power broker who alternately allied himself with and then betrayed Afghans, Soviets, and the Taliban. He was considered a ruthless warlord with a strong power base."[20]

During the next several days, American Special Operations Forces, trained by the most powerful and sophisticated military in the world, rode on horseback. They traveled into the craggy local mountains surrounding Mazar-i-Sharif and scouted Taliban positions. The Americans saw that the enemy was clearly not prepared to fight a modern war. Many rode in open pickup trucks armed only with Soviet-made AK-47 assault rifles known as Kalashnikovs. They had no uniforms and possessed primitive communications equipment such as two-way radios or walkie-talkies.

Because the enemy was nearby, Task Force Dagger called in close air support. This tactic is used to target enemies who are in close proximity to friendly forces—in this case the American fighters on the ground. The use of close air support required Team Dagger to be in constant communication with B-1 bombers and F/A-18 Hornet fighter jets. When targets were identified, the bombers swooped in and took out the targets.

From October 24 to November 7, Task Force Dagger used close air support to destroy Taliban military vehicles, key command posts, bunker positions, ammunition storage facilities, and antiaircraft artillery. The bombs also caused hundreds of casualties among Taliban fighters. Some survivors decided to change sides and join the Northern Alliance. Other fighters escaped into the Pashtun tribal region in Waziristan, located in northwestern Pakistan.

Between air strikes, Dostum's forces and Team Dagger conducted old-style cavalry charges, riding at the enemy with guns blazing. According to Stewart, "During these attacks SOF team members were in the forefront of the action, often on horseback, even though only one member of the team had ever ridden extensively before."[21] By November 10 the Taliban were in complete disarray, with survivors fleeing in panic. Dostum and his fighters rode into the center of Mazar-i-Sharif, to the cheers of local residents. With the fall of the Taliban in the region, the US-led coalition experienced its first victory in the Afghan war. Coalition forces now controlled a strategic stronghold in northern Afghanistan, along with a major airport in Mazar-i-Sharif.

The Collapse of the Taliban

Even as Team Dagger fought for control of Mazar-i-Sharif, around two hundred US Army Rangers and other special operations forces parachuted into Kandahar in southern Afghanistan. Kandahar was the birthplace of the Taliban movement, but it easily fell as the rangers, assisted by heavily armed AC-130 Spectre gunships, conducted raids in the area. On the night of November 12, Northern Alliance forces began what was planned to be a multiday, five-phase operation to take Kabul. However, when coalition forces arrived the next day, they found only bomb craters, burned out buildings, and abandoned Taliban gun placements. Taliban and al Qaeda leaders, and possibly Osama bin Laden, had slipped away in the dark of night. Within twenty-four hours coalition forces also took control of Afghanistan's other major cities, including Herat, Jalalabad, and Kunduz. On November 25 about one thousand US Marines flew into the desert south of Kandahar, ferried in by massive CH-53E Super Stallion helicopters. The marines set up Camp Rhino, the first forward operating base, or military base used to support tactical operations.

When defeat appeared inevitable, Mullah Omar called for the Taliban to fight to the death. However, on December 6 Taliban leaders called a truce and promised to surrender to coalition forces. Rather than die fighting, Omar slipped out of Kandahar surrounded by a group of loyalists in a convoy of motorcycles.

Two weeks later, a temporary government was put in place in Afghanistan until democratic elections could be held. Only seventy-eight days had passed since combat operations began. However, as history professor Terry Anderson writes, "It was a laser-fast victory with few allied casualties, yet the world now wondered: where was Osama bin Laden?"[22]

Bin Laden at Tora Bora

The CIA learned Bin Laden was in Jalalabad on November 14. The terrorist mastermind was among hundreds of Taliban and al Qaeda fighters fleeing coalition forces. However, by the time CIA teams arrived, Bin Laden had escaped to Tora Bora, a network of natural caves located in some of the most rugged terrain in the world. The caves were located in the White Mountains south of Jalalabad in eastern Afghanistan, near the Pakistan border.

American intelligence officials long suspected that al Qaeda had dug bunkers and built training camps in and around Tora Bora. There was speculation in the media that Bin Laden was hiding deep within Tora Bora. The hideout was described in British and American newspapers as a multitiered lair carved into the solid rock by the Bin Laden family's construction company. The lair was purportedly filled with weapons and protected by two thousand fanatical al Qaeda guards.

B-1 Bombers in Afghanistan

The US military possesses the most advanced aircraft in the world. Many of the bombers and fighter jets were originally designed and built to fight the Soviet Union, a former superpower that no longer exists. For example, the supersonic B-1 with a 7,450 mile (11,990 km) range, was built to drop nuclear bombs on distant targets. In 2001 the plane was repurposed for fighting the Taliban.

The current model B-1, originally designed in the 1970s, flew more than one thousand missions a year during the Afghan war. Each plane was capable of carrying several dozen 2,000 pound (907 kg) smart bombs. These powerful bombs were guided by Global Positioning Systems that could hit targets with a high degree of accuracy. In Afghanistan the B-1 would stay in the air and circle, with no specific targets. If troops on the ground needed bombs delivered, the plane could reach speeds of 830 miles per hour (1,336 kph), arriving on the scene very quickly. In addition to its bombing capabilities, the B-1s were equipped with highly sensitive sensors that constantly scanned the ground. The sensors could detect groups of Taliban fighters or even a single insurgent planting improvised explosive devices (IEDs).

With the ability to fly in all weather and at high or low altitudes, the versatile B-1 was used on 72 percent of all combat missions in Afghanistan after 9/11. According to a 2003 statement by US Air Force secretary James Roche, "It is entirely appropriate for us to suggest that the B-1, as we employ it today, is transformational."

Quoted in Armed Services Committee, "The B-1 Bomber: A Critical Asset of the Long Range Strike (LRS) Mission," 2010. http://armedservices.house.gov.

On December 3 the CIA was able to pick up the sound of Bin Laden's voice on a walkie-talkie and pinpoint his location in Tora Bora. Gary Berntsen ordered an airstrike, hitting the site with a 15,000-pound (6,804 kg) BLU-82 bomb, one of the largest nonnuclear bombs ever used. The BLU-82 is called the "daisy cutter," an ironic name since it can flatten an entire forest and thus allow helicopters to land. Although the bomb killed countless al Qaeda fighters, Bin Laden and his deputy Ayman al-Zawahiri managed to survive.

Coalition forces in Tora Bora prepare C-4 explosives to be used on bunkers and caves in the region. For a time, US intelligence sources believed Bin Laden and his al Qaeda training camps were located there.

Four Battle Plans

By December 5 Northern Alliance fighters were encamped on the low ground beneath Tora Bora. The Jawbreaker team was also there, backed by special operations forces from the army's Delta Force. The Americans were calling in air force strikes, which pounded the area night and day. However, there was a disagreement among American officials concerning the best way to capture Bin Laden. Berntsen believed al Qaeda had at least one thousand fighters in Tora Bora. He sent a detailed message to CIA headquarters requesting an army ranger battalion of eight hundred soldiers to assault the cave complex and block escape routes to the Pakistan border, which was only about 6 miles (10 km) away.

Brigadier General James Mattis, who was in command of eleven hundred marines at Camp Rhino, had his own plan. Mattis wanted to move his troops to Tora Bora and seal off the border to Pakistan. He also called for the air force to drop hundreds of land mines on the mountain passes that led out of Afghanistan, which would make any al Qaeda escape attempts nearly impossible.

Delta Force members formulated an idea for an unconventional attack. The army fighters wanted to scale the 14,000-foot (4,267 m) peaks of the White Mountains above al Qaeda's positions wearing oxygen masks so they could operate in the thin mountain air at high elevations. Thus equipped, Delta Force would mount a deadly attack on al Qaeda positions below.

Despite the numerous plans for catching Bin Laden, Tommy Franks was instructed to carry out orders dictated by Bush and Cheney. The official US policy was to allow local tribesmen to capture Bin Laden, backed by tactical support from a team of about forty special ops forces. According to the Bush administration, the Pakistan Army would join the effort, amassing on the border to prevent Bin Laden and members of the Taliban and al Qaeda from escaping Afghanistan. However, there were problems with the official plan. Despite promises by Pakistani president Pervez Musharraf to seal the border, satellite surveillance photos showed no Pakistani soldiers in the region, which left all escape routes open.

Another problem involved the Northern Alliance fighters, who were ill-prepared to take on al Qaeda at Tora Bora. The three militia leaders in the area intensely disliked one another. The troops under their command quarreled constantly and even exchanged gunfire at times. In addition, it was bitterly cold, and the indigenous fighters were poorly equipped. Some were wearing only sandals as they trudged through snow-covered mountain passes. CIA official Hank Crumpton was monitoring the situation at Tora Bora from Washington, DC. As he explained to Bush: "[The Afghan fighters are] tired and cold and many of them are far from home. They're just not invested in getting bin Laden."[23]

Eight Days of Fighting

The Battle of Tora Bora began on December 12, 2001. The beginning of the assault is described by Stewart: "After a short trip in the ubiquitous pickup trucks, the teams were forced to unload and move forward on foot with burros carrying their packs. Moving into mountains where the altitude varied from 10,000 to 12,000 feet, they progressed slowly over rocky and narrow paths."[24]

Over the course of five days and nights, the fight took on a kind of rhythm. During the day the Northern Alliance fighters engaged the enemy. Al Qaeda fought back with its arsenal of rockets, machine guns, and artillery. At night the local militias fell back while the US Air Force pummeled the mountain peaks and canyons. The air force eventually dropped 700,000 pounds (317,515 kg) of bombs from F-18s, F-14s, and B-1 bombers. Hundreds of al Qaeda soldiers were killed. Finally, the fighting stopped when both sides wearied.

On December 13 an al Qaeda leader negotiated a truce with local militia commanders. This turned out to be a ruse. It was later learned that when combat had halted, Bin Laden escaped into Pakistan. Fighting soon flared again, but it was a rearguard action, taken to hold off the militia while al Qaeda and Taliban leaders fled into Pakistan. Omar and al-Zawahiri were among those who got away.

Coalition forces were finally able to enter Tora Bora on December 17. They found no massive bunkers, only a few small outposts with minor

The Myth of the Tora Bora Lair

In late November 2001 it was widely believed that Osama bin Laden was living in a high-tech headquarters dug into the caves of Tora Bora. The rumor was perpetuated by the British and American media and given credence by Defense Secretary Donald Rumsfeld. The myth of the Tora Bora lair began on November 27 when correspondent Richard Lloyd Parry of the British newspaper the *Independent* wrote that al Qaeda was almost "immune to attack inside its hi-tech underground lair . . . [which] has its own ventilation system and its own power, created by a hydro-electric generator. Its walls and floors in the rooms are smooth and finished and it extends 350 yards beneath a solid mountain." Without naming a source for this wild claim, Parry stated that the site extended deep underground (the equivalent of a one-hundred-story building) and housed two thousand al Qaeda fighters in hotel-like comfort. On November 29 the *Times* of London published a cutaway drawing of the purported underground lair.

The Associated Press picked up the story in the United States. It was published with the drawing by newspapers, magazines, and websites. On December 2 Rumsfeld appeared on the TV show *Meet the Press* and confirmed the existence not only of the underground Tora Bora hideout but also of many other such locations. However, the fantastic story collapsed several weeks later when US forces finally took control of Tora Bora. They found no underground fortress, no hydroelectric power plant, and no hotel rooms. The high-tech Tora Bora lair of Bin Laden turned out to be a myth.

Quoted in Edward Jay Epstein, "Fictoid #3: The Lair of Bin Laden," Netherworld, 2013. www.edwardjayepstein.com.

training camps. Bin Laden was nowhere to be seen. According to CIA estimates, there were about 220 dead militants and 52 captured fighters.

The "Gravest Error"

Berntsen blamed Franks and CENTCOM for the missed opportunity to capture Bin Laden in Afghanistan. Most Americans were unaware of the situation until April 17, 2002, when the *Washington Post* revealed for the first time that Bin Laden had been present at Tora Bora. The article, which quoted government and military officials, concluded that the Bush administration's failure to commit ground troops to hunt Bin Laden was the "gravest error of the war against al Qaeda."[25]

Administration critics blamed Bin Laden's escape on the military's unconventional war strategy, which relied on local fighters and small teams of American forces. In December 2001 there were only 350 Special Operations Forces, 110 CIA officers, and 4,000 marines in all of Afghanistan. This small number of personnel was called upon to fight and secure a country of around 26 million people. The number of troops in Afghanistan was less than the number of police officers in New York City, Chicago, or Los Angeles. With most troops holding positions in Kandahar and Kabul, the military lacked a sufficient number of soldiers to win Tora Bora.

After Bin Laden's escape, the president changed his tone about the al Qaeda leader. By mid-March 2002 Bush avoided mentioning Bin Laden. When questioned by reporters, Bush stated: "Terror is bigger than one person. He's a person that's now been marginalized. . . . [Bin Laden has] met his match and may even be dead. I truly am not that concerned about him."[26]

Relief Efforts

Whatever the fallout from Tora Bora, Americans and their allies had much to celebrate in late 2001. The Afghan people had been liberated from the repressive Taliban and the al Qaeda terrorists were gone. However, the country was now without a formal government. To remedy that situation, the United Nations Security Council convened a conference on December 5 in Bonn, Germany. The conference created what was called the Bonn Agreement, officially known as the Agreement on Provisional Arrangements in Afghanistan Pending the Re-establishment of Permanent Government Institutions.

The Bonn Agreement created a temporary government, called the Afghan Interim Authority, which would rule Afghanistan until democratic elections could be held. Hamid Karzai was named chair of the interim government. Karzai was a college-educated Pashtun who spoke several languages. During the Soviet war, Karzai worked as a covert CIA agent and acted as a fund-raiser for the mujahideen. He also provided intelligence to special forces after the war began in October 2001.

Another measure of the Bonn Agreement created the International Security Assistance Force (ISAF), which consisted of military forces from the United States, Canada, Australia, and several European nations, including the United Kingdom, Germany, France, Denmark, and Netherlands. The main purpose of the ISAF was to create and train the Afghan National Army and to secure Kabul and the surrounding area.

Beyond setting up a new government, the international community acted to provide aid to the Afghan people. The relief organization World Food Programme was able to deliver enough food in December 2001 to feed 6 million Afghans during the following two months. In addition, the United Nations raised nearly $400 million for emergency relief in 2012. However, the United Nations estimated that Afghanistan would require $10 billion over ten years, including $1.3 billion to cover immediate needs.

Operation Anaconda

Even as world leaders made plans for a postwar Afghanistan, small pockets of dedicated Taliban and al Qaeda fighters remained active in the countryside. By this time the American military had established a central command force at Bagram Air Base north of Kabul. Throughout February 2002 Bagram filled with newly arrived special forces, including Task Force K-BAR made up of US Navy SEALs and elements of the

Third Special Forces Group (Airborne) out of Fort Bragg in North Carolina. Before long the number of US-led coalition troops in Afghanistan grew to around ten thousand.

In March special forces teams discovered a major contingent of two hundred to five hundred experienced Taliban and al Qaeda fighters in the Shahi Kot Valley in eastern Afghanistan. This enemy force was thought to be about as large as the one at Tora Bora. Like Tora Bora, the combatants were dug into fortified caves high in the mountains. The coalition plan to deal with the enemy in Shahi Kot was code-named Operation Anaconda. Unlike at Tora Bora, coalition commanders were not going to rely mostly on local fighters. The Anaconda team consisted of more than one thousand army troops from the Tenth Mountain Division (Light Infantry) and the 101st Airborne Division. Operation Anaconda also employed special forces fighters from the United Kingdom, Canada, Australia, Germany, Denmark, and France. Around

Canadian soldiers move through the Shahi Kot Valley in eastern Afghanistan in March 2002. Coalition forces experienced many problems in the fight for control of this valley.

seven hundred Northern Alliance fighters, led by a man known as Zia, joined this group. (Many Afghans go by a single name.)

The Shahi Kot Valley is long and narrow and surrounded by 11,000-foot (3,353 m) mountains. There are only two roads in and out of the valley, and most of the trails are goat paths. With its forbidding terrain, the valley proved to be a difficult battlefield. The primary mission of Anaconda was to surround the valley and prevent enemy fighters from leaving, a strategy called isolation and encirclement. This would be followed by attacks to capture or kill the trapped Taliban and al Qaeda fighters.

Friendly Fire

The fight for control of the Shahi Kot Valley began at midnight on March 2, and things went wrong from the start. The convoy carrying the main coalition of about forty fighters, called Task Force Hammer, became bogged down while driving on a muddy, winding road into the valley. One of the trucks overturned and several got stuck. As the convey ground to a halt, troops on the ground spent precious hours trying to extract the vehicles. Some trucks were abandoned, which forced soldiers to pile onto those that still worked, dangerously overloading the vehicles. Many soldiers were forced to set out for battle on foot.

The troops soon came under fire from a helicopter circling above. One American and two Afghans were killed, and twelve to fifteen were wounded. A subsequent investigation showed that the gunfire was "friendly fire" from an American aircraft that shot at the troops after mistaking them for the enemy. The friendly fire reduced Task Force Hammer to about half its original members. The movements of the remaining fighters were easily observed by Taliban and al Qaeda fighters entrenched on ridges high above the valley. The enemy rained down mortar and machine-gun fire as coalition helicopters tried to evacuate the wounded. The momentum of the attack ground to a halt. Stewart picks up the story:

> [The] planned U.S. air strikes that were to assist Zia were poorly coordinated and generally ineffective. Expecting a hail of bombs, Zia's men watched as only a handful hit enemy positions on the

[mountain], causing no slackening in enemy mortar and artillery fire. Commander Zia and his men initially held up well, but after many hours of enemy bombardment with no way to answer back and ineffective or nonexistent close air support, their morale began to suffer.[27]

"A Long, Difficult Struggle"

While Task Force Hammer struggled, coalition forces in other areas were assaulted by heavy enemy fire. Withering battles throughout the valley continued for days. The heaviest coalition casualties occurred when six Americans were killed on March 4 on Takur Ghar, a mountain to the southeast of the valley. During the days that followed, wind and fog slowed coalition air support as the troops worked their way across various ridgelines, clearing caves and enemy positions along the way. Al Qaeda fighters were able to use their familiarity with the terrain to mask their positions and movements.

Operation Anaconda lasted until March 19, when coalition forces finally took total control of the Shahi Kot Valley. The battle resulted in large caches of weapons and ammunition being seized. A great deal of valuable intelligence was discovered in papers and notebooks left behind in cave hideouts. The operation was declared a success because an estimated one hundred to one thousand al Qaeda fighters had been killed. However, an unknown number of enemy fighters had escaped into the Pakistani tribal regions.

Although it was unknown at the time, Operation Anaconda was an indicator of things to come. The terrain and the weather worked against the US-led coalition. At the same time, the coalition was not prepared for the ferocity and tenacity of the enemy that engaged them. Despite the coalition casualties and the frustrating arc of the battle in the Shahi Kot Valley, most Americans and Europeans considered Operation Enduring Freedom a success. By the spring of 2002, an estimated three thousand to four thousand Taliban fighters had been killed, about seven thousand taken prisoner, and almost all of the al Qaeda training camps and other facilities destroyed. About one-third of Taliban leaders and half of al Qaeda leaders were believed dead.

While American politicians and military leaders claimed victory, Berntsen was not so sure. As he flew out of Afghanistan in 2002, the CIA leader wrote:

> To the credit of our President, our government and the citizens it serves, we'd responded to an attack on our shores with intelligence, drive and strength. But we'd failed to finish the job. I understood that this was just the end of the first chapter in a long, difficult struggle against al-Qaeda and other terrorist organizations that we would have to wage diplomatically, culturally and militarily throughout the world.[28]

Chapter 3

The Taliban Resurgence

In June 2002 there was great optimism in the United States about the progress of the Afghan war. With coalition forces controlling Kabul, Kandahar, Jalalabad, and other cities, it seemed as if victory was assured. This would allow the United States to return control of Afghanistan to its people. However, toppling the Taliban had created a power vacuum that was quickly filled by warlords. Some were traditional mujahideen, and others were newly rich, financed by the CIA and US military to fight the Taliban.

The situation in Afghanistan was complicated by the fact that the main agricultural crop was—and remains—the poppy. This flower produces opium, which is refined into heroin, a highly addictive substance. About 10 percent of Afghans, most of whom are desperately poor, are involved in opium cultivation. The bulk of Afghanistan's heroin is sold in Europe and the United States. Many Afghan warlords maintained their wealth and power producing and transporting this destructive drug.

The drug trade also benefited the Taliban, which controlled large swaths of land in Helmand, Kandahar, and other opium-producing provinces along the Pakistan border. The insurgents commandeered fruit orchards and vegetable fields and turned them into poppy fields. This allowed the Taliban to reap great profits from opium production but also reduced the amount of food grown in a country where millions were lacking proper nutrition.

With billions of dollars in drug profits at stake, drug producers often clashed violently, killing innocent civilians in the process. As a result, there was a feeling of general lawlessness in the countryside in mid-2002. This prompted Afghan's interim leader, Hamid Karzai, to request twenty thousand additional US-led coalition troops to police the countryside.

A Secondary Theater of War

Even as Karzai was asking for an increased US presence, the George W. Bush administration was secretly making plans for the war in Iraq. Planning and prosecuting this war would steer American military resources away from Afghanistan. These resources included intelligence and surveillance capabilities, the skills of special forces and conventional troops, and tens of billions of dollars.

On March 19, 2003, the United States staged a massive invasion of Iraq in order to depose its leader, Saddam Hussein. The war, code-named Operation Iraqi Freedom, was much larger than the one in Afghanistan. It was initially conducted with 148,000 troops from the United States, 45,000 from the United Kingdom, 2,000 from Australia, and 194 from Poland.

Hussein was deposed within weeks of the initial invasion, and his military force was defeated. On May 1 Bush made a dramatic speech on the aircraft carrier USS *Abraham Lincoln* and declared victory in Iraq under a banner that read "Mission Accomplished." However, in the months that followed, the Iraqi resistance increasingly targeted American soldiers, using automatic weapons, mortars, rocket-propelled grenades, car bombs, sniper attacks, and other guerrilla tactics. It soon became clear that American leaders had underestimated the strength of the enemy, and the mission of bringing stability to Iraq was far from accomplished. As the situation deteriorated, it riveted the attention of the American public and world media, which pulled reporters from Afghanistan to cover the war in Iraq.

Afghanistan was left with a small contingent of about eleven thousand US and international troops. Their focus was humanitarian assistance and supporting the interim government. In military parlance, Afghanistan was known as a secondary theater of war. In practice this meant that the American commitment in Afghanistan took a backseat to events elsewhere, leaving the military effort to languish while resources were diverted to Iraq.

Despite diminished fighting capacity, coalition military operations were needed to root out Taliban and al Qaeda insurgents. Coalition troops were also training new recruits to the Afghan National Army (ANA), which was by this time receiving money and weapons from the United States. In addition, coalition forces were called upon to collect heavy weapons left behind by the Taliban and stem fighting between clashing warlord factions. As a result, several coalition operations were conducted in the summer of 2003.

Afghan National Army soldiers, patrolling in Kandahar province, encounter a field of poppies in bloom. About 10 percent of Afghans cultivate opium poppies, which are used in the making of heroin.

From Warrior Sweep to Avalanche

In July the coalition initiated Operation Warrior Sweep to kill or capture enemy fighters believed to be active in the mountain valleys of Paktia Province. About one thousand ANA soldiers led the operation, assisted by the US Eighty-Second Airborne Division, which flew troops into the area in CH-47 Chinook helicopters. The forces encountered no Taliban fighters but did discover around twenty thousand military weapons hidden in secret caves.

Several other 2003 coalition efforts, including November's Operation Mountain Resolve and December's Operation Avalanche, produced similar results. Some enemy fighters were killed, but most escaped, and small to medium weapons caches were captured. Although the operations proved to be largely futile, they were punishing to coalition forces. Operating in deep snow and steep, rough terrain, troops were forced once again to use pack mules to transport heavy equipment.

Renewing the Struggle

In October 2004 Karzai was elected president in Afghanistan's first democratic election. By this time Taliban fugitives were recruiting soldiers from the Pashtun population along the Afghanistan-Pakistan border, an area known as the Taliban heartland. Small, mobile training camps, with up to two hundred fighters each, were built with heroin profits and money from so-called charity donors in Saudi Arabia who were sympathetic to the Taliban cause. Al Qaeda leaders were running the camps and training Taliban fighters in guerrilla warfare and terrorist tactics, including suicide attacks. The ultimate goal was to renew the struggle against the US-led coalition and the Karzai government.

Throughout 2004 the insurgents conducted sporadic raids, ambushes, and rocket attacks on American soldiers, civilians, government officials, and humanitarian workers. However, the main Taliban efforts did not begin until the summer of 2005 when Mullah Omar established a fighting force called the Quetta Shura Taliban, based in the city of Quetta, Pakistan. Omar divided Afghanistan into five operational zones, each with its own Quetta Shura commander who coordinated a national strategy against coalition forces.

Night Letters

The reemergence of the Taliban was attributed to at least two major factors. One was the inability of the Afghan government to establish a strong presence throughout the country. The second was the failure of coalition forces to secure and stabilize rural areas of the country. This allowed the Taliban to establish "shadow" control in nearly half of the nation's thirty-four provinces, especially those bordering Pakistan.

In order to spread its violent, extremist message in Pashtun tribal areas, the Taliban began sending out what were called *shabnamah*, or "night letters." These letters or leaflets were posted in public places at night and warned villagers against cooperating with US forces, referred to as "Christian invaders."[29] Those who ignored the night letters could expect swift and violent retribution. One message from the Taliban (who referred to themselves as the Mujahidin) was written over a drawing of a large knife:

> We Mujahidin received information that you and your son are working for Americans. You cannot hide from Mujahidin, we will find you. If you and your son do not stop working for Americans then we will cut you and your son's heads with the knife that you see in this letter. Anybody who is working with the American will be punished with the knife that you see in this letter.[30]

Night letters were sent to people seen driving government vehicles or simply talking to coalition soldiers. Teachers were also targeted. The United States had implemented a program of building schools for girls and young women. This policy was violently opposed by the Taliban. In 2005 a night letter posted on a tree in Kapisa Province stated, "This is a warning to all those dishonorable people, including . . . teachers, not to teach girls. . . . We strongly ask those people whose

Planning the War in Iraq

The invasion of Iraq was on the agenda of the George W. Bush administration even before the terrorist attacks of September 11, 2001. Iraq was ruled by Saddam Hussein, a brutal dictator. Hussein had invaded Kuwait in late 1990, sparking the Persian Gulf War. The US military quickly ejected Iraq from Kuwait. However, in 1998 Hussein killed five thousand of his own people with chemical weapons because he believed they were threatening his power. In the following years there were suspicions—but no proof—that Hussein was building weapons of mass destruction that could be used by terrorists targeting the United States.

Almost immediately after Bush became president in January 2001, his administration secretly began planning a war with Iraq. The plans were interrupted by 9/11; a month after the attack, Vice President Dick Cheney appeared on *Meet the Press*. Cheney alleged there had been direct links between Hussein and al Qaeda for more than a decade. Critics pointed out that Osama bin Laden and Hussein were enemies, but Cheney continued to repeat the charge. This claim was eventually debunked by the independent 9/11 Commission, formed in November 2002 to prepare a complete account of the circumstances surrounding the September 11 attacks. According to the commission report, "We have no credible evidence that Iraq and al-Qaeda cooperated on attacks against the United States." Despite this, a *Washington Post* poll showed 70 percent of Americans mistakenly believed Hussein was responsible for 9/11 when the war in Iraq began in 2003.

Quoted in NBCNews.com, "9/11 Panel Sees No Link Between Iraq, al-Qaida," June 16, 2002. www.nbcnews.com.

Afghan girls attend school. In the Taliban view, the education of girls is an act of evil deserving of death.

names have been particularly reported to us, not to commit this act of evil. Otherwise, it is they who bear all the responsibilities."[31] Three days later the Kapisa girls' school was burned to the ground. Malim Abdul Habib, the headmaster of Shaikh Mathi Baba High School, which educated both boys and girls in Zabul Province, was stabbed eight times and decapitated after receiving a similar night letter in January 2006.

Improvised Explosive Devices

While night letters were used to intimidate civilians, a second terror tactic was aimed at coalition forces and their ANA allies. The first attack with an IED occurred in Iraq on March 29, 2003, just ten days after the US invasion. The bomb, made of more than 100 pounds (45 kg) of C-4 plastic explosive, was detonated in the trunk of a taxi cab carrying several US soldiers. After that first detonation, the technology for roadside bombs, suicide bombs, and vehicle-borne bombs was brought by Iraqi insurgents to Afghanistan.

By 2004 the IED was the signature weapon in Afghanistan. Triggering mechanisms and explosive materials such as ammonium nitrate fertilizer were imported from Pakistan. In 2004 there were 300 IED attacks in Afghanistan. In 2005 there were 500 IED bombings; by 2007 that number had increased to 2,677. These bombs were the number one killer of US troops in Afghanistan, responsible for about half of all combat casualties in the country.

A typical IED terrorist cell in Afghanistan consisted of six to eight people, including a financier who bought the materials, a bomb maker, a person who placed the bomb, and a spotter who alerted a triggerman when a target approached. A cameraman was often there to shoot a video of the exploding US vehicles and bloody Americans. These gruesome videos were posted on the Internet by the Taliban to win new supporters. Former deputy assistant secretary of defense Joseph J. Collins analyzed the situation: "With a priority on operations in Iraq, the United States was surprised at the virulence of the Taliban attack that began in earnest."[32]

To establish countermeasures to IEDs in Afghanistan and Iraq, the Defense Department established the Joint IED Defeat Organization, or JIEDDO. Anti-IED technologies included electronic jammers, which used low-power radio signals to stop the devices from detonating, and predetonators to blow up the bombs before targeted vehicles arrived. Robots also proved to be useful. The Talon was a robot known as an unmanned ground vehicle. It was equipped with a mechanical arm to inspect and relocate suspected IEDs. Another device, the Pack-Bot, was used to clear bombs and explore suspected booby traps in terrorist hideouts. The military also redesigned transport vehicles, giving them a V-shaped hull, which dispersed the force of an explosion and kept the vehicle from flipping over.

These measures did not come cheaply. Between 2004 and 2006 anti-IED research, development, and acquisition of countermeasure tools cost the United States $6.1 billion. And despite this massive funding effort, coalition injuries and casualties from IEDs in Afghanistan and Iraq continued to mount.

Operation Mountain Thrust

With Taliban attacks escalating in early 2006, Lieutenant General Michael Maples, director of the Defense Intelligence Agency, warned Congress that the insurgents "represent a greater threat [to the pro-US government] than at any point since late 2001."[33] Despite this warning, the United States began drawing down its troop presence in order to divert military resources to Iraq. As a result, the United Nations–created International Security Assistance Force (ISAF) took responsibility for military operations in southern Afghanistan in January 2006. The bulk of the ten-thousand-member force consisted of US conventional forces, British troops from the Sixteenth Air Assault Brigade and the Royal Marines, and Canadian and Dutch soldiers. They were aided by several hundred fighters from Denmark, Australia, and Estonia. The ISAF was also joined by several thousand troops from the ANA.

The coalition's main mission was to stop the growing violence in southeast Afghanistan near the Pakistan border. In this region, according to reporter Paul Wiseman, the Taliban were "ambushing military patrols, assassinating opponents and even enforcing the law in remote villages where they operate with near impunity."[34] In addition, the ISAF hoped to disrupt the opium trade, run by profiteers who helped finance the Taliban.

In May 2006 the ISAF and ANA launched Operation Mountain Thrust in the Panjwai District in Kandahar Province, the site of numerous IED attacks. Panjwai is considered the spiritual homeland of the Taliban, and it borders Helmand Province, where 75 percent of the world's opium is produced.

Coalition forces scoured Kandahar and Helmand for around seven weeks. They battled about two thousand Taliban insurgents in sixteen known firefights, the fiercest fighting since Operation Enduring Freedom began in 2001. Allied artillery bombardments and airstrikes eventually turned the battle in favor of the ISAF. By the time the operation ended on July 11, coalition forces had suffered 155 casualties, including 24 Americans, 4 Canadians, 11 Australians, and 107 Afghans from the ANA. More than 1,100 insurgents were killed, and 400 were captured.

US forces used vehicles with a V-shaped hull like this one to plow through mine fields of C-4 explosives in Afghanistan. Improvised explosive devices made from C-4 became the signature weapon in the war.

"Disunity of Effort"

About one month after the conclusion of Operation Mountain Thrust, Canadian troops launched Operation Medusa to clear the area of Taliban fighters. The Canadians were met by violent retaliation from an estimated two thousand insurgents, who engaged them in gun battles and hit them with ambushes and mortar and rocket attacks. It took weeks of fighting before the Panjwai District was secured. Twelve Canadians were killed, along with 512 insurgents. Although the insurgents suffered a high number of casualties during the two operations, Tom Koenigs, the top United Nations official in Afghanistan, warned that this did not reflect success: "The Taliban fighters' reservoir is practically limitless. The movement will not be overcome by high casualty figures."[35]

Koenigs's words proved to be prophetic. Various ISAF forces engaged the insurgents throughout the rest of 2006 and discovered that the Taliban refused to give ground. In the south and east, Operations Mountain Fury, Wyconda Pincer, and Falcon Summit all resulted in bloody battles, coalition injuries and casualties, and high fatalities among the insurgents. While temporary victories were achieved, the Taliban were not defeated.

By the end of 2006, the Afghan war was going badly, and political support for the effort was collapsing in coalition nations. Citizens were questioning whether the effort was worth the blood and expense. Diplomats and military leaders from member nations of the ISAF were blaming one another for the situation. As military historians John R. Ballard, David W. Lamm, and John K. Wood write, "The violence and diplomatic chaos caused a great deal of finger-pointing but did little to advance a coalition military effort that was by that time hamstrung by . . . disunity of effort."[36] Insurgent leaders were well aware of the disunity and believed all they had to do was wait until the Americans and Europeans decided it was time to go home.

Poppy Eradication

In an effort to reduce casualties among coalition ground troops fighting in rough terrain, the ISAF dramatically increased bombing campaigns. Coalition forces dropped nearly 2,650 tons (2,404 metric tons) of bombs in 2006, more than thirty times the tonnage dropped in 2004. In 2008 that number nearly doubled again to 5,050 tons (4,581 metric tons). Although this airpower damaged the enemy, it also killed civilians. By 2006 more than four thousand noncombatants had been killed in Afghanistan. While exact figures are unknown, an estimated 25 percent of those died during coalition bombing campaigns.

Civilian deaths hurt coalition efforts to win the allegiance of average Afghans. Winning their allegiance, or winning the hearts and minds of the population as it is sometimes stated, involved digging wells, providing medicine, and distributing food to the 70 percent of Afghans who were chronically malnourished. However, coalition food relief programs were poorly executed and failed to provide much relief even as bombs rocked the country on a daily basis. This prompted the London-based think tank the Senlis Council to write that the bombing campaigns "fan the Taliban flame. The Taliban present these policies as evidence to their compatriots of the foreigner untrustworthiness. According to this message, foreigners are waging a war against the people of southern Afghanistan; the US and its allies are on a quest of global domination, whose ultimate goal is the destruction of Islam."[37]

Another source of contention was centered on the coalition goal of eradicating poppies. Beginning in 2006 joint missions involving US Special Forces, US Drug Enforcement Administration special agents, and the Afghan military and police were conducted in Helmand Province. Labs where heroin was refined were destroyed, and large drug caches were seized. In addition, Afghan authorities destroyed poppy fields, pulling out the plants before they were ready to harvest. However, these manual eradication efforts only destroyed about 5 percent of the total poppy acreage and did little to win allegiance. Poppy cultivation is strongly rooted in the social, political, and economic culture of Afghanistan. In the harsh mountain climate, poppies are one of the only sustainable crops. As the Senlis Council explains, "Poppy eradication alienates rural communities from the Karzai administration and drives them into the hands of the Taliban. These policies provide [the Taliban with] recruitment opportunities among ruined farmers whose crops have been eradicated, and who seek revenge for the destruction of their livelihoods."[38]

Like other aspects of US involvement in Afghanistan, the antidrug efforts proved futile. According to a report by the United Nations Office on Drugs and Crime, the Taliban only got about 5 percent of the estimated $3 billion generated annually by opium production in Afghanistan. While this was still a large amount, most of the Taliban's money came from non-opium sources, such as private donations. Farmers received only about 20 percent of the opium money, while the rest went to traffickers, government officials, the police, and local warlords. Making matters worse, opium production in Afghanistan skyrocketed from 185 tons (168 metric tons) in 2001 to 6,100 tons (5,534 metric tons) in 2006 and 8,200 tons (7,439 metric tons) in 2007. When coalition forces wiped out poppy fields and destroyed heroin labs, they created a drug shortage. This caused prices to rise dramatically, which spurred farmers to plant even more poppies to take advantage of the higher prices.

Opium Addiction in Afghanistan

Afghanistan has produced around 90 percent of the world's opium for decades, and much of that is processed into heroin that is sold in countries from India to the United States. Opium production makes up about one-third of Afghanistan's economy and fuels widespread corruption. Although the media often reported on these topics, what was often ignored was the effect cheap, readily available opium had on average Afghans. CNN senior international correspondent Ben Wedeman describes the situation:

> If you want to see the devastating impact of opium on Afghan society, just go to Kabul's main stadium any day of the week. There, you'll find dozens of men and teenagers, huddled against the wall, inhaling opium fumes or shooting up heroin. The ground is strewn with used needles.
>
> There I met Shafiqallah, a man in his 30s—although he looked 20 years older—who has been addicted to opium for the last six years. . . . He told me he begs for the money to pay for his $4-a-day habit, plus feed his wife and six children. In Afghanistan, the average daily per capita income is less than $2. . . .
>
> The number of opium addicts in Afghanistan has skyrocketed in recent years. In 2005 it was estimated that there were 900,000 addicts in the country. Three years later that number had jumped to 1.5 million. It's not clear why the number of heroin addicts has spiked in recent years, but Afghan officials are hoping their efforts to eradicate opium . . . will help curb the use of the drug.

Ben Wedeman, "Afghanistan's Curse: Opium," *Afghanistan Crossroads* (blog), CNN World, February 22, 2010. http://afghanistan.blogs.cnn.com.

Operation Achilles

The war on drugs and the war on the Taliban continued throughout 2007. Between March and May joint Afghan-ISAF operations were conducted in Helmand Province under the code name Operation Achilles. With more than fifty-five hundred troops, the operation was promoted to the Western media as the largest multinational joint forces operation launched to date. It was undertaken during the height of the poppy harvesting season and was meant to drive Taliban forces out of the troubled province.

When coalition forces arrived on March 16, there were few enemy fighters to be found. Village elders had asked the Taliban to leave so they could conduct their harvest without coalition planes dropping bombs on their fields. The Taliban largely complied with the request. However, there were heavy firefights in late April when coalition forces engaged several hundred Taliban fighters around the village of Girishk, killing 130. This battle triggered a massive public protest in the region, with local villagers claiming the dead were civilians defending their homes. Operation Achilles was more successful in mid-May when coalition fighters killed Mullah Dadullah, second in command of the Taliban.

Two American soldiers were killed during Operation Achilles, and the United Kingdom and Canada each suffered six casualties. These deaths and the ongoing battles in Afghanistan were hardly noted in the American media, whose attention was focused on Iraq. There, in July 2007 alone, insurgents conducted 1,666 IED attacks. In Afghanistan, things were little better as the year ended. According to a Pentagon report compiled in January 2008, "The Taliban has regrouped after its initial fall from power in Afghanistan [and has] coalesced into a resilient insurgency. The Taliban is likely to maintain or even increase the scope and pace of its terrorist attacks and bombings in 2008."[39]

Around the time the Pentagon released its report, Bush predicted both wars would continue after his second term ended in January 2009. Although war was assured, no one could predict the outcome of the situation in Afghanistan.

Chapter 4

The Surge

In 2008 Afghanistan was wracked by violence. In April Hamid Karzai barely escaped an assassination attempt as gunmen opened fire during a military parade. In July fifty-eight people were killed when the Indian Embassy in Kabul was blasted by a suicide car bomber. This was one of many spectacular suicide bombings throughout the year that killed hundreds of civilians, government officials, and coalition soldiers in Kabul, Kandahar, and elsewhere.

One of the bloodiest battles of the war took place on July 13, 2008. Several hundred Taliban and al Qaeda fighters launched a coordinated attack with automatic weapons and rocket-propelled grenades on a remote US base in Wanat. Within the first twenty minutes of the attack, nine US troops were killed and twenty-seven wounded, out of forty-eight defending the base. The outnumbered coalition forces prevailed in the end, but the base was abandoned after the fight.

New President, Old Wars

On November 4, 2008, as Afghanistan descended into chaos, Americans elected a new president. In the run-up to the election, Barack Obama promised to redouble America's efforts in Afghanistan and end the war in Iraq. However, by the time Obama took the oath of office on January 20, 2009, most Americans were not thinking about Afghanistan. The US economy was foundering in the worst economic recession since the 1930s. Millions of people had lost their jobs in the previous year, and the real estate market was near collapse. During his inauguration speech, Obama spoke at length about the financial hardships faced by Americans and outlined broad plans to save the economy. He only mentioned the wars he was inheriting once: "We'll begin to responsibly leave Iraq to its people and forge a hard-earned peace in Afghanistan."[40]

While Obama did not dwell on America's wars during his speech, he issued an executive order on his first day in office. The US military was to make plans to withdraw all combat troops from Iraq. Obama was able to order this action in part because of steps taken by George W. Bush in January 2007. Faced with the prospect of defeat in Iraq, Bush had ordered what was called a surge—deployment of an additional twenty thousand American soldiers. By the time Obama was sworn in, there was general agreement that the surge had worked. Violence in Iraq was down, the country was stabilized, and the US-backed government was able to operate with greater freedom. The time had come for the United States to leave Iraq.

Afghanistan, meanwhile, remained a secondary theater of war despite an increasing level of violence. A total of 295 coalition members were killed in Afghanistan in 2008, including 155 Americans. About 60 percent of those fatalities were caused by IED attacks, which numbered 3,276. In addition, 795 Americans were wounded in 2008.

Deciding on a Strategy

During his first months in office, Obama often visited wounded soldiers in the Walter Reed Army Medical Center in Washington, DC. After one such visit, the president referred to Afghanistan when he told one his advisers, "I don't want to be going to Walter Reed for another eight years."[41]

During the presidential election campaign, Obama had promised to send in more troops to reinforce the 38,000 Americans and 30,000 allied forces already in Afghanistan. In March 2009 Obama made good on that promise, deploying an additional 21,000 troops. However, this number was about half the 40,000 soldiers requested by General Stanley A. McChrystal, the new commander in charge of the war.

By increasing the number of troops, Obama was hoping to ensure a smooth presidential election in Afghanistan in August 2009. Karzai was seeking a second term, and coalition troops were tasked with preventing the Taliban from attacking voters, polling places, and candidates. However, by this time Karzai was deeply unpopular and widely blamed for failing to stop violence against average citizens. Karzai was also seen as very corrupt. In 2009 the organization Transparency International rated Afghanistan the second-most corrupt nation in the world. It did not help

Afghan president Hamid Karzai (pictured) barely escaped an attempt on his life when gunmen opened fire on a military parade in 2008. Others were not so lucky, as suicide bombings became a regular tactic of insurgents.

Karzai's cause that his younger brother, Ahmed Wali Karzai, was alleged to be controlling the opium and heroin trade.

Karzai was reelected in August in an election tainted by allegations of fraud. While the Obama administration had hoped that Karzai would help the United States advance America's interests, the compromised Afghan president came to be viewed as a burden rather than an asset.

Meanwhile, according to CIA reports, the Taliban were steadily growing in power and threatening to take over most of Afghanistan. One of the signs of the Taliban's increasing strength was the growing number of US troop casualties. July 2009 was the deadliest month in the eight-year war for American fighters and their allies. Roadside bombs, rocket attacks, and ambushes, combined with aviation accidents, killed forty-three Americans and seventy-two coalition troops, including twenty-two British soldiers. The increased combat casualty count was attributed to the growing US troop forays into Taliban-dominated areas. By the end of 2009, a total of 255 Americans had died in Afghanistan, a 43 percent increase over 2008.

As the death toll mounted, McChrystal renewed the call for a troop surge and warned of Afghanistan "mission failure."[42] The general concluded it would take 500,000 soldiers five years to gain an upper hand in Afghanistan. However, opinion polls showed that only 32 percent of Americans approved of a major troop increase.

In November 2009 Obama reached something of a compromise. He announced he was sending an additional 30,000 American troops to initiate an Afghanistan surge. The ISAF agreed to send an additional 7,000 troops, and by the summer of 2010 McChrystal was commanding a security force totaling around 100,000. For the first time since 2003, the number of US troops in Afghanistan outnumbered those in Iraq.

Clear, Hold, Build

The surge strategy was summarized in three words: *clear, hold, build.* Coalition forces would clear troubled regions of insurgents and hold the areas so the insurgents did not return. Meanwhile advisers would help build a working society so that young men had other options

Weapons in hand, Taliban fighters look confident from their perch atop a tank in Kandahar. By 2009, the Taliban was steadily growing in power and threatening to retake control of Afghanistan.

besides fighting for the Taliban. Clear, hold, build differed from the strategy of earlier years when American forces would clear an area of Taliban fighters then leave, allowing the insurgents to return. The old method was derisively referred to by American soldiers as "mowing the grass."[43]

Mowing the grass failed because most Taliban fighters were not motivated by political or religious beliefs but by money; the Taliban paid soldiers about one hundred dollars a month. This was a good wage in a nation where most people earned little over one dollar a day. As Secretary of State Hillary Clinton explained in 2009, the focus of the United States would be to "lure the people away from the Taliban with offers of participating in society, paying them if necessary, having a job and a future that is better than the Taliban offers."[44]

The Civilian Surge

The clear, hold, build strategy was first put to the test in February 2010 when the US Marines and the ANA confronted the Taliban in the city of Marjah. As part of the new strategy, the coalition forces publicly announced their intention to invade the city and encouraged insurgents to leave before the operation started. Many of them did, thereby avoiding violence. In this operation, the ANA proved to be a valuable fighting force, identifying Taliban members who were hiding in Marjah during a house-to-house sweep of the town.

After Marjah was secured, coalition forces set up a security ring around the town to prevent the Taliban from coming back, as had happened in previous years. The next step was meant to help the locals build normal lives. People were paid for homes that were damaged in the sweep, and Americans met with elders to build trust and open lines of communication. A group of newly trained ANA personnel was flown in to provide policing and other services. Local civilians were offered jobs on projects ranging from building schools, markets, and health clinics to digging irrigation canals. Agricultural advisers were brought to the area to show farmers how to grow wheat, vegetables, and fruit in the now-fallow opium fields.

The coalition then moved on to the Taliban heartland of Kandahar, where it also implemented the clear, hold, build strategy. But while soldiers on the ground were holding and building, a different form of war was being waged from the air.

Drone Strikes

As part of the surge, the Pakistani military agreed to help coalition forces drive the Taliban out of the tribal areas along the Afghanistan-Pakistan border, sometimes referred to as Af-Pak. At the time, the United States was providing Pakistan with more than $1 billion in military aid annually. Some of this money went to Pakistan's Inter-Services Intelligence (ISI) spy agency, which often worked against American interests. According to electronic surveillance and US informants, powerful members of the ISI supplied the Taliban with money, military supplies, and strategic planning. When confronted with this information, Pakistani president Asif Ali Zardari promised to sever all ISI ties to the insurgents.

Ongoing doubts about Pakistan's willingness to adhere to the US agenda led to an increase in the use of drone strikes in the Af-Pak region. Drones, also known as unmanned aerial vehicles, were first used by the CIA in Pakistan in 2004 to kill an insurgent named Nek Muhammad Wazir. At the time, the existence of drones and their use in war remained top secret information known only to high-ranking military personnel and US government officials. In the years that followed, drones played a growing role in the war. Most drones used in Afghanistan were operated from a base in Tampa, Florida. Drone pilots viewed potential targets through video cameras that were attached to the underside of the craft. The vehicles were controlled by joysticks, like those used in video games. The drones could stay aloft for twenty-four hours at heights of up to 25,000 feet (7,620 m). The Reaper drone carried fourteen deadly laser-guided supersonic Hellfire missiles, which deliver a 100 pound (45 kg) bomb designed to penetrate bunkers and destroy tanks.

Between 2006 and 2010 an estimated two thousand insurgents were killed by missiles fired from drones in Af-Pak. About half of those deaths occurred in 2010 when Obama ordered 122 drone strikes. While the missile strikes were officially top secret, a growing number of eyewitness reports surfaced concerning civilians killed by secondary strikes. For example, in May 2009 a CIA drone hit a group of Taliban officials in the village of Khaisor, killing at least a dozen people. Villagers joined surviving Taliban members as they rushed to aid the wounded and retrieve the dead for burial. As the rescuers dug through a bombed home, a follow-up attack was launched, with two drone missiles killing twenty-nine people, at least half of them civilians.

Funerals for drone victims were also targeted by the CIA in order to kill Taliban leaders who attended the processions. This occurred in June 2009, after Taliban commander Khwaz Wali Mehsud was killed in a drone strike along with five others. According to Chris Woods and Christina Lamb of the London-based nonprofit Bureau of Investigative Journalism, "Up to 5,000 people attended Khwaz Wali Mehsud's funeral that afternoon, including not only Taliban fighters but many civilians. US drones struck again, killing up to 83 people. As many as 45 were civilians, among them reportedly ten children and four tribal leaders."[45] On such occasions, the military made payments of $2,900 to civilians who were wounded by drones and $4,800 to the families of innocents who were killed.

Villagers gather near the remnants of a house destroyed in an apparent drone strike. Drones have been instrumental in killing Taliban and al Qaeda fighters, but many such attacks have also resulted in civilian deaths.

The Afghan War Diary

On July 25, 2010, the secrecy surrounding drones and many other aspects of the Afghan war was wiped away. More than ninety-one thousand classified US military and intelligence reports, known as the Afghan War Diary, were posted online by WikiLeaks, an organization that publishes restricted and confidential material from anonymous sources. The documents also appeared on the websites of the *New York Times,* the British newspaper the *Guardian*, and the German newspaper *Der Spiegel*. The Afghan War Diary logs were, according to the US government, illegally downloaded by Private First Class Bradley Manning, an army computer specialist who worked with classified military databases in Iraq. Manning said he was troubled by many aspects of the war, including the number of civilian deaths; his supporters labeled him a whistleblower concerned about government abuses. However, the army did not see Manning as a do-gooder. In 2013 he was convicted of twenty criminal charges, including six violations of the Espionage Act. The judge in the case acquitted him of the far more serious charge of aiding the enemy. In August 2013 Manning was sentenced to thirty-five years in prison.

The Afghan War Diary was the largest leak of confidential information in US military history. The military logs revealed details compiled between January 2004 and December 2009 about the deaths of Afghan civilians and the extensive involvement of Pakistan and Iran in the insurgency. According to a July 2010 article in the *New York Times*, the documents offer

> an unvarnished, ground-level picture of the war in Afghanistan that is in many respects more grim than the official portrayal. The secret documents . . . are a daily diary of an American-led force often starved for resources and attention as it struggled against an insurgency that grew larger, better coordinated and more deadly each year. . . . [The documents] illustrate in mosaic detail why, after the United States has spent almost $300 billion on the war in Afghanistan, the Taliban are stronger than at any time since 2001.[46]

Perhaps one of the most telling statements in the Afghan War Diary was a sarcastic comment by Vice President Joe Biden. Referring to

Shedding Light on Afghanistan

When WikiLeaks published more than ninety-one thousand classified military and intelligence reports online in July 2010, the documents provided details about the Afghan war that were largely hidden from the public. The *New York Times* published some of the major points:

> The Taliban have used portable heat-seeking missiles against allied aircraft, a fact that has not been publicly disclosed by the military. This type of weapon helped the Afghan mujahedeen defeat the Soviet occupation in the 1980s.

> Secret commando units like Task Force 373—a classified group of Army and Navy special operatives—work from a "capture/kill list" of about 70 top insurgent commanders. These missions, which have been stepped up under the Obama administration, claim notable successes, but have sometimes gone wrong, killing civilians and stoking Afghan resentment.

> The military employs more and more drone aircraft to survey the battlefield and strike targets in Afghanistan, although their performance is less impressive than officially portrayed. Some crash or collide, forcing American troops to undertake risky retrieval missions before the Taliban can claim the drone's weaponry.

> The Central Intelligence Agency has expanded paramilitary operations inside Afghanistan. The units launch ambushes, order airstrikes and conduct night raids. . . .

> Sabotage and trickery have been weapons every bit as potent as small arms, mortars or suicide bombers. So has Taliban intimidation of Afghan officials and civilians—applied with pinpoint pressure through threats, charm, violence, money, religious fervor and populist appeals.

C.J. Chivers et al., "View Is Bleaker than Official Portrayal of War in Afghanistan," *New York Times*, July 25, 2010. www.nytimes.com.

the complex nature of the war in Afghanistan, Biden said, "Besides the demography, geography and history of the region, we have a lot going for us."[47] He was referring to the fact that Afghanistan is known as the "Graveyard of Empires" because no great power, including England in the nineteenth century and the Soviet Union in the twentieth, ever won a war in the harsh mountain terrain against fierce Pashtun resistance.

The Battle for Kandahar

That resistance was on display less than a year after the Afghan War Diary was published. On May 7, 2011, the insurgents launched what they called the Taliban spring offensive against Afghan security forces and government officials. The main Taliban target was Kandahar, which had been in the hands of coalition forces for about a year. Launched less than a week after US Navy SEALs killed Osama bin Laden, the offensive was meant to show that the Taliban were still a fearsome fighting force. According to an official Taliban statement, "Operations will focus on attacks against military centers, places of gatherings, airbases, ammunition and logistical military convoys of the foreign invaders in all parts of the country. . . . All Afghan people should bear in mind to keep away from gatherings, convoys and centers of the enemy so that they will not become harmed during attacks of Mujahideen against the enemy."[48] The message also warned of multiple suicide attacks, referred to as collective martyrdom operations.

The battle for Kandahar began in the early morning when about one hundred militants attacked the provincial governor's office with rocket-propelled grenades, guns, and other weapons. The insurgents later trained their weapons on police stations, government offices, and other buildings. The strikes were coordinated with suicide bombers, who simultaneously killed at least four civilians and wounded fifty.

The Afghan National Police engaged the fighters, and after several days of combat nearly all the insurgents were killed or captured. However, the bloody offensive continued. On May 16 a suicide car bombing in Kabul killed six American soldiers and nine Afghans. In mid-June several suicide attacks, including one by a bomber pushing an ice-cream cart filled with explosives, killed at least twenty-one people, including eight children, in Kandahar.

Nation Building at Home

On June 22, as violence continued in Afghanistan, Obama gave a nationally televised speech from the White House. He announced that with the killing of Bin Laden on May 1, the United States would reduce its role in the region. Obama announced that the United States would be removing ten thousand troops from Afghanistan by the end of 2011 and bringing home an additional thirty-three thousand by the summer of 2012. This would mark the end of the surge. The president told the nation that the United States would end all combat operations in Afghanistan and bring home all troops by 2014. Obama stated: "We will not try to make Afghanistan a perfect place. We will not police its streets or patrol its mountains indefinitely. . . . Over the last decade, we have spent a trillion dollars on war at a time of rising debt and hard economic times. Now, we must invest in America's greatest resource: our people. . . . America, it is time to focus on nation building here at home."[49]

Deadly Incidents

Even as the president promised to end American involvement in Afghanistan, the fighting continued. On August 6, 2011, the Taliban shot down a US Chinook helicopter attempting to provide combat aid to a unit of army rangers fighting in Wardak Province, west of Kabul. The crash killed all thirty Americans aboard, including seventeen members of SEAL Team 6, the unit that had killed Bin Laden. (None of the seventeen had actually participated in that operation.) Military analysts concluded that the hit on the helicopter was simply a lucky shot on the part of the Taliban. However, that did little to alleviate the fact that it was the single deadliest incident against American troops in the history of the war.

In September the Taliban continued with its lethal offensive, carrying out several high-profile attacks during a five-day period. A suicide bomber blew up his truck on a coalition base in Wardak Province, wounding seventy-seven Americans and killing four ANA soldiers. Insurgents attacked the US embassy, an ISAF base, and the police station in Kabul, killing eleven civilians.

Death of Osama bin Laden

Osama bin Laden evaded the CIA for nearly nine years. During this period he continued to direct al Qaeda terrorist attacks throughout the world. The terrorist mastermind was finally traced to Abbottabad, Pakistan, after the CIA followed an al Qaeda messenger to Bin Laden's hideout in August 2010. The CIA had known about the courier for four years but could not previously locate him.

At 1:00 a.m. on May 1, 2011, a team of twenty-four US Navy SEALs carried out the CIA mission code-named Neptune Spear. The assault on Bin Laden's compound was closely monitored by Barack Obama in the White House Situation Room via live video feeds streamed from commandos' helmet cameras. Neptune Spear was carried out without alerting the Pakistani government for fear that someone would notify Bin Laden. The SEALs flew in from Jalalabad, Afghanistan, in two Black Hawk helicopters, a ninety-minute flight taken close to the ground to avoid detection. After arriving, the SEALs gained entrance to Bin Laden's compound by blowing off doors and breaching walls with explosives. The SEALs encountered Bin Laden in a residential area, where he lived with his family. Fearing he was armed, one of the SEALs shot him in the head, killing the world's most wanted terrorist. The next day Bin Laden's body was loaded on the aircraft carrier USS *Carl Vinson* and buried in the north Arabian Sea.

Meanwhile, average Afghans continued to suffer. In October the Karzai government asked the World Food Programme for $142 million to feed 2.6 million faced with starvation. One of the worst droughts in a decade had ravaged crops in half of the nation's districts. October also saw opium production surging 60 percent over the previous year, despite intensified eradication efforts.

Insider Attacks

On May 1, 2012, exactly one year after the killing of Bin Laden, Obama flew to Bagram Air Base in Kabul. The president and Karzai signed a strategic partnership agreement that outlined cooperation between the United States and Afghanistan for ten years following the coalition withdrawal. The agreement also made clear that Afghans would be responsible for their own security. However, the United States promised to provide billions of dollars to train the Afghan National Security Forces, which consisted of the Afghan National Army and the Afghan National Police.

Like much else in Afghanistan, the Afghan National Security Forces training program did not work as planned. Insurgents began infiltrating the Afghan military and police forces where American military trainers were working. When the opportunity presented itself, the infiltrators detonated suicide vests or opened fire with small arms. About twenty insider attacks occurred between 2009 and 2011, and that number more than doubled to forty-six in 2012. At least sixty-three coalition troops—most of them Americans—were killed, and eighty-five were wounded. The deaths accounted for 15 percent of all coalition casualties in 2012.

In August Mullah Omar released a statement concerning the insider attacks, referring to the Taliban as the Mujahideen and exaggerating the effectiveness of the strikes: "Thanks to the infiltration of the Mujahideen, they are able to (safely) enter bases, offices and intelligence centers of the enemy. Then, they easily carry out decisive and coordinated attacks, inflicting heavy losses on the enemy both in life and equipment."[50]

The insider attacks continued. On May 4, 2013, an Afghan soldier opened fire on coalition troops, killing two Americans in what was the sixth insider attack of the year. The same day five US soldiers were killed in Kandahar by an IED. With more than eighteen months left before Americans left Afghanistan, the death toll kept climbing.

Chapter 5

What Was the Impact of the War in Afghanistan?

When the United States launched a war on terrorism after the September 11, 2001, attacks, it was clear to most Americans who the enemies were—Osama bin Laden, his al Qaeda followers, and the Taliban government protecting them in Afghanistan. A majority of Americans, around 90 percent, supported the invasion of Afghanistan in 2001. However, after the Taliban were defeated during the initial combat phase in 2002, the war became nearly invisible to the American public.

By 2010, even as US military personnel fought and died in Afghanistan, only 25 percent of Americans said they closely followed news about the war, according to the Pew Research Center for the People and the Press. This lack of interest was reflected in another Pew study, which showed the Afghan war accounted for less that 4 percent of the nation's news coverage that year. As media critic John Hanrahan commented in 2011, "The war without end is a war with hardly any news coverage."[51]

Multiple Tours of Duty

Most Americans did not feel much impact from the Afghan war because few were called upon to fight in it. About 2.5 million Americans—well under 1 percent of the population—volunteered to serve in the military while the war was being waged. An even smaller number, about half a million, were deployed to Afghanistan, with average deployments lasting nine to fifteen months. About 70 percent of all US troops who served in Afghanistan were also deployed to Iraq.

Many soldiers served multiple deployments. For example, army staff sergeant Bobby Martin Jr. fought a total of four combat tours in Afghanistan and Iraq between 2003 and 2010. Martin saw five of his men killed, four of them in Afghanistan in 2010. Thirty-eight cumulative months in combat left him with bad knees and recurring headaches caused by a roadside bomb.

Martin and many other soldiers in the twenty-first century made military history: They had served in combat longer than any other soldiers in any other American war. The combat tours were so long and so frequent that more than 13,500 soldiers spent four cumulative years at war, about the entire length of America's involvement in World War II. By comparison, the vast majority of Americans who fought in Vietnam between 1964 and 1972 had served a single one-year tour of combat duty.

The Effect on Veterans

Multiple tours of duty increased the chances that a soldier could be killed, and the suffering spread far beyond the battlefield. More than 2,245 US troops were killed in Afghanistan, and those who died left about 22,300 grieving family members behind. More than 18,000 were wounded in action, and tens of thousands of family members have been left to care for injured veterans, some of whom suffered traumatic brain injuries, multiple amputations, and other severe wounds caused by IEDs.

The psychological toll of war left a lasting mark on many veterans. One in five vets, or more than 250,000 who served between 2001 and 2013, suffer from post-traumatic stress disorder (PTSD) or depression. Vanessa Williamson and Erin Mulhall, policy directors of the organization Iraq and Afghanistan Veterans of America, describe PTSD and depression:

> PTSD is a psychological condition that occurs after an extremely traumatic or life-threatening event, and has symptoms including persistent recollections of the trauma, heightened alertness, nightmares, insomnia, and irritability. Major depression

can include persistent sadness or irritability, changes in sleep and appetite, difficulty concentrating, lack of interest, and feelings of guilt or hopelessness.[52]

These traumas, also known as invisible wounds, took their toll in many ways. Research links increased alcohol consumption with veterans suffering from combat-related illnesses. In addition, according to the Costs of War website, those suffering from invisible wounds see "increased drug dependence, higher rates of violence including homicide and child abuse and neglect . . . high risk behaviors that have re-

A soldier talks with a physician's assistant at Fort Hood in Texas. The military has made efforts to help returning service members deal with the events and feelings they experienced both during and after their deployments.

sulted in elevated numbers of car crashes and drug overdoses, elevated levels of homelessness and divorce."[53]

Homelessness, in particular, is a vexing problem among those suffering from depression and PTSD. In 2012 the US Department of Veterans Affairs reported that more than 26,530 veterans of the wars in Afghanistan and Iraq were living on the streets of America. As Randy Brown, a spokesperson for the National Coalition for Homeless Veterans, explains, "Making a transition to civilian life—readjusting to family, getting a job or education—after multiple combat tours may not come easily and could have delayed consequences."[54]

The burdens of war have also driven hundreds of veterans to suicide. According to the Veterans Health Administration, in 2013 veterans accounted for 20 percent of all US suicides—about twenty-two a day. About half of those veterans served in the twentieth century and were over the age of fifty. However, veterans between the ages of seventeen and twenty-four—those who served after 9/11—had suicide rates four times higher than other veterans. In addition, suicide among active-duty troops rose steadily over the course of twelve years and two wars, reaching 350 in 2012. That surpassed the number of troops killed in Afghanistan that year.

Like so much else about the Afghan war, much of the suffering remained invisible to average citizens. After marine Clay Hunt committed suicide following the trauma of seeing his friends die in Afghanistan, his mother stated, "The Marines are at war and America's at the mall."[55]

Impact on Average Afghans

The suffering of average Afghans was also largely unseen by most Americans; news of civilian hardship and death received even less media coverage than the war in general. However, the armed conflict touched nearly everyone in Afghanistan. Those simply trying to live out their daily lives were trapped between the insurgents and the coalition forces in a war fought among the civilian population. As a result, an estimated seventeen thousand to twenty-two thousand civilians died of war-related injuries from 2001 to 2013.

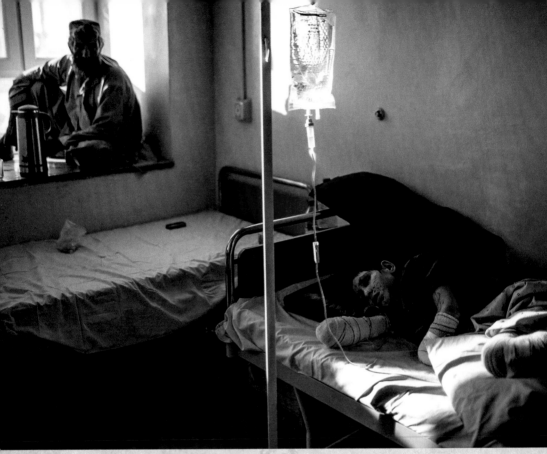

A twelve-year-old Afghan boy lies in a hospital bed. He faces an uncertain future after losing both arms and a leg when he triggered an improvised explosive device while playing outside his home.

Civilians were killed by crossfire, assassination, bombing, and coalition raids into houses of suspected insurgents. The indiscriminate use of IEDs was the biggest civilian threat. Some of these devices were made to explode when stepped on, and the crude land mines often killed children and others walking along roadsides. Removal of unexploded devices by coalition forces was hampered by the insurgents, who beat, mutilated, or killed those who attempted to report the location of IEDs.

Taken as a whole, the situation explained the pessimistic attitude most Afghans had about the future. In 2006 an ABC News/*Washington Post* poll showed 67 percent of Afghans believed coalition forces would bring stability to their country. By 2011 that number had dropped to 31 percent.

Financial Costs

As the human suffering in Afghanistan continued, the financial costs also mounted. The US military spent about $1 million to support each individual soldier in Afghanistan for a year. In 2011, during the surge, the entire war effort cost roughly $6.7 billion a month, or $80.4 billion for the year. The total cost of the war in Afghanistan between 2001 and 2013 was almost $700 billion. (The cost of the war in Iraq was around $813 billion.)

The costs of fighting these two wars did not include future obligations to more than 1 million veterans. These obligations include paying for medical expenses and disabilities at least through 2050. In 2013 a Harvard University study predicted both wars will eventually cost between $4 trillion and $6 trillion. According to Linda Bilmes, who coauthored the study, "The single largest accrued liability of the wars in Iraq and Afghanistan is the cost of providing medical care and disability benefits to war veterans. Historically, the bill for these costs has come due many decades later."[56]

In the past the United States paid for wars by raising taxes and selling war bonds to the public. However, the wars in Afghanistan and Iraq were paid for almost entirely by borrowing $2 trillion, much of it from China. This was a significant component of the $9 trillion US deficit accrued after 2001. As Bilmes and economist Joseph Stiglitz write, "The legacy of poor decision-making from the expensive wars in Afghanistan and Iraq will live on in a continued drain on our economy—long after the last troop returns to American soil."[57]

The Ongoing War on Terror

The use of American drones to kill terrorists throughout the world is another legacy of the Afghan war. Even as combat operations ended in the Af-Pak region, the CIA continued launching drone strikes in the area. However, the number of strikes fell dramatically to only one or two a month as the war wound down. The Obama administration justified the drone strikes by citing the Authorization for Use of Military Force Against Terrorists (AUMF) passed by Congress three days after

Solemn Statistics

Most American soldiers who fought in Afghanistan also served one or more tours of duty in Iraq. In March 2013, as the war in Afghanistan was winding down, journalist James Wright provided some solemn statistics about the two wars the United States fought after 9/11:

> Over 6,660 U.S. servicemen and women have died in these wars—145 have been women. Over 1,000 of these men and women were under 20 years of age; more than 3800 were 25 or younger (fatalities in Iraq were on average younger than those in Afghanistan.) The survivors' organization TAPS has estimated that the wars in Iraq and Afghanistan have left 3,659 widows and widowers with 4,790 surviving children, 13,306 grieving parents and 19,559 grandparents. Since 2001, 18,311 Americans have been wounded in Afghanistan. And 32,223 were wounded in Iraq between 2003 and 2011. These only count the visible wounds.

> Of course, these wars have impacted people beyond our borders, as well. There have been 619 casualties from the United Kingdom and 780 from other coalition countries—most of these have died in Afghanistan. And the United Nations has reported that in the years 2007–2013 14,728 Afghan civilians lost their lives as a result of the war (in the last year it is estimated that over 80 percent of these were due to anti-government forces.)

James Wright, "Have Americans Forgotten Afghanistan?," *Atlantic*, March 25, 2013. www.the atlantic.com.

9/11. The AUMF gave the American president unprecedented powers to wage war in Afghanistan and elsewhere. It remained the legal foundation of most counterterrorist operations in 2013, twelve years after the bill was passed. And the list of targets continued to grow.

After being driven out of Afghanistan, al Qaeda began recruiting in Yemen, Mali, Libya, Somalia, and Syria. While few of these al Qaeda offshoots were known to possess the money or tactical skills to strike at the United States, Barack Obama justified targeting leaders for drone attacks. In a May 2013 speech on drone policy, Obama said: "We are at war with an organization [al Qaeda] that right now would kill as many Americans as they could if we did not stop them first. So this is a just war—a war waged proportionally, in last resort, and in self-defense."[58] This concept troubled critics like Illinois senator Richard Durbin, who stated in June 2013: "None of us, not one who voted for [the AUMF], could have envisioned we were voting for the longest war in American history, or that we were about to give future presidents the authority to fight terrorism as far-flung as Yemen and Somalia."[59]

Guantánamo Bay Detainee Camp

The AUMF was also used by the US government as a legal justification to capture, interrogate, and jail suspected terrorists—and hold them indefinitely without trial. The center of this activity was the Guantánamo Bay detention camp located at the Guantánamo Bay Naval Base in Cuba, or Gitmo, as it is widely known. The prison, opened in January 2002, was established to hold Taliban and al Qaeda leaders and other prisoners of war captured in Afghanistan and elsewhere. The location was chosen because Guantánamo, being in Cuba, is not subject to US laws. This means prisoners held there are not guaranteed access to American courts. Within a year of its opening, the Gitmo detention camp held more than 740 prisoners captured in Afghanistan. These men were from all parts of the world, including the United Kingdom, Yemen, Denmark, Somalia, Morocco, Pakistan, and even China.

Donald Rumsfeld called the Gitmo prisoners "the worst of the worst,"[60] and there were several high-value detainees at Gitmo, including Khalid

Sheikh Mohammed, the principal architect of 9/11. However, many detainees were low-level combatants or civilians caught in the wrong place. According to a 2006 report by the Center for Policy and Research, about 80 percent of Gitmo prisoners were not captured on the battlefield but were exchanged for bounty payments. In the early weeks of the war, the United States posted leaflets promising a $5,000 reward, a huge sum to average Afghans, for the capture of Taliban or al Qaeda terrorists.

The story of Shaker Aamer is typical of what happened after a bounty was offered for terrorists in Afghanistan. Aamer, a Saudi native, was a British resident who once lived in the United States. When the 9/11 attacks occurred, he was in Afghanistan doing charity work, digging wells and building a girls' school in Kabul. After the US invasion Aamer was captured by the warlords of the Northern Alliance and sold to the US military for a $5,000 bounty. Aamer ended up a prisoner in Gitmo, where he remained in 2013, living in a tiny, windowless cell. Aamer was among hundreds of average citizens—including cab drivers, farmers, and other prisoners—who were never charged with a crime. One Gitmo detainee was fourteen years old when he was captured. According to Colonel Lawrence B. Wilkerson, who served in the George W. Bush administration as a senior official in the State Department with access to classified documents, many of the prisoners detained at Guantánamo Bay were taken into custody "without regard for whether they were truly enemy combatants, or in fact whether many of them were enemies at all."[61]

Another controversial practice at Gitmo was called enhanced interrogation by the Bush administration, and torture by critics. Whatever the term, some prisoners at Gitmo were subjected to sleep deprivation, prolonged exposure to extreme temperatures, and simulated drowning, or waterboarding. According to a 2005 CIA memo, Mohammed was waterboarded 183 times after he was captured in Pakistan in 2003. CIA officials were hoping that Mohammed would lead them to Bin Laden and reveal plans for new terrorist acts.

A Recruiting Tool for Terrorists

In 2008, when Barack Obama ran for president, he promised to close down Gitmo within a year if elected. However, members of Congress

The Kajaki Dam Fiasco

The United States spent at least $100 billion on relief and reconstruction projects in Afghanistan between 2002 and 2013. Some of this money was stolen, wasted, or mismanaged, according to special inspector general John Sopko, who investigated spending by the US Agency for International Development (USAID). One example of wasted money was the Kajaki Dam project in the troubled Helmand Province. USAID had hoped that improvements to the dam would provide electricity to a region of 1.7 million residents, most of whom have never experienced the benefits of reliable electric power.

In 2005 American planners decided to improve the hydroelectric dam with a new power turbine that would boost electricity production. USAID paid a Chinese contractor an unreported sum to install the turbine. However, the region was so dangerous that the project was temporarily put on hold. In the summer of 2008, with the Taliban still in the area, the British conducted a six-day military operation with four thousand troops to transport the new turbine to Kajaki Dam. However, the Chinese engineers abandoned the project because of Taliban kidnapping threats.

In 2010 USAID tried again, awarding $266 million to an American construction company to finish the dam. By mid-2013 the Kajaki Dam project was still incomplete, and the Taliban continued to fight any attempt to fix the dam, according to a statement by Qari Yusuf Ahmadi: "We will never let the Americans do anything here. . . . They never do anything which is good for Islam."

Quoted in Jean MacKenzie, "Watershed of Waste: Afghanistan's Kajaki Dam and USAID," GlobalPost, October 11, 2011. www.globalpost.com.

want to keep the prison open and continued to place restrictions on the transfer of Guantánamo Bay prisoners to US prisons or to foreign countries. As of May 2011, six hundred detainees had been released from Gitmo. As of June 2013, 166 prisoners remained in the camp, designated to be detained indefinitely without trial. That month the House of Representatives passed a bill to keep the infamous prison open. Even as the bill was passed, the remaining prisoners engaged in a hunger strike, protesting their incarceration.

Critics maintain that the existence of Gitmo has had a negative impact on the status of the United States throughout the world. As constitutional lawyer Scott Roehm writes, "The prison continues to undermine our moral standing in the world and to damage our relationships with allies; the financial cost is astounding, at nearly $1.6 million per detainee annually; and—as the most powerful symbol of abuses committed by the United States in the post-9/11 era—Guantanamo serves as a recruiting tool for [terrorists] who wish to do us harm."[62]

The Taliban Remain a Threat

Twelve years after the United States first went to war in Afghanistan, many aspects of life there had changed, but much remained the same. The Taliban no longer ran the government, but they remained a powerful force in the country. For example, they revived their campaign to destroy educational opportunities for Afghanistan's girls and young women.

During the course of the war, the United States spent $1.9 billion on education for girls in Afghanistan. This money paid for building or refurbishing schools, paying teachers, and enrolling students. During this time school enrollment for girls rose from around 5,000 in 2001 to 2.5 million in 2012, according to the Afghan Education Ministry. However, attending school continued to be a dangerous pursuit for girls in Afghanistan. The Taliban threatened and intimidated girls and their teachers. In 2012 alone there were at least 185 documented attacks on Afghan girls' schools, according to the United Nations. In April 2012 militants poisoned more than one hundred schoolgirls in northern Afghanistan because they defied an order to stay home. The girls, while sickened, survived. Several months later, an insurgent threw a grenade into a girls' school in Kandahar, killing one hundred students.

"Almost Nothing Has Changed"

In other areas of life, progress has also been slow. Kabul, with 3.3 million residents, is the only capital city in the world without a modern sanitation system. The roads are unpaved, and raw sewage flows through ditches next to new clinics and schools built by the West. Political corruption is rampant. Schools and clinics were built with shoddy materials, while the contractors pocketed most of the money. Politicians used their positions to steal public land, siphon aid money for personal use, and protect criminal enterprises. Civil servants such as the police continue to demand bribes.

In addition to corruption, terror attacks and suicide bombings by insurgents create widespread anxiety. In 2012, 56 percent of Afghans said they often or sometimes fear for their own personal safety or that

With the help of a donkey, an Afghan farmer brings in his wheat harvest. Despite years of war, life for ordinary Afghans in the countryside has changed little.

of their family. A similar number said they were fearful when voting. Three-quarters of those polled said they had a fear of traveling from one part of the country to another. Only 24 percent replied that they are never afraid.

In the countryside the lives of average Afghans seem to remain frozen in time. Journalist Anna Badkhen, who spent a great deal of time in Afghanistan between 2001 and 2013, explains: "Most of the hinterland has remained unchanged. The electricity, the sanitation, the clean water, and education has not really reached most of Afghanistan. It's a very rural country, and in the rural areas, almost nothing has changed since 2001. Since 2000 years ago, much of Afghanistan lives the same way."[63]

Source Notes

Introduction: The Defining Characteristics of the War in Afghanistan

1. Arianna Huffington, "Afghanistan: Our Longest and Least Talked About War," *Huffington Post*, October 10, 2012. www.huffington post.com.
2. Quoted in Thomas Nagorski, "Editor's Notebook: Afghan War Now Country's Longest," ABC News, June 7, 2010, http://abc news.go.com.
3. Quoted in Justine Elliot, "Biden's One-Sentence Summary of the Afghan War," *Salon*, December 2, 2010. www.salon.com.

Chapter One: What Events Led to the War in Afghanistan?

4. Quoted in Terry H. Anderson, *Bush's Wars*. New York: Oxford University Press, 2011, p. 70.
5. Quoted in Anderson, *Bush's Wars*, p. 62.
6. Quoted in Anderson, *Bush's Wars*, p. 64.
7. Osama bin Laden, "Text of Fatwah Urging Jihad Against Americans," Wayback Machine, 2006. http://web.archive.org.
8. Quoted in John Miller, "Interview: Osama bin Laden," *Frontline*, 2013. www.pbs.org.
9. Quoted in CNN, "Bin Laden Says He Wasn't Behind Attacks," September 17, 2001. http://archives.cnn.com.
10. Quoted in *Frontline*, "Forming a 'Mighty Coalition,'" 2013. www.pbs.org.
11. Quoted in John R. Ballard, David W. Lamm, and John K. Wood, *From Kabul to Baghdad and Back*. Annapolis: Naval Institute Press, 2012, p. 32.
12. Quoted in William Boardman, "America's 'Permanent War': The 'Authorization to Use Military Force' Forever," Global Research, May 26, 2013. www.globalresearch.ca.
13. Quoted in Anderson, *Bush's Wars*, p. 81.

14. Quoted in Tim Russert, "Text: Rumsfeld on NBC's 'Meet the Press,'" *Washington Post*, September 30, 2001. www.washington post.com.

15. George W. Bush, *Decision Points*. New York: Crown, 2010, p. 187.

16. Gary Berntsen and Ralph Pezzullo, *Jawbreaker*. New York: Crown, 2005, p. 75.

17. Quoted in Ballard, Lamm, and Wood, *From Kabul to Baghdad and Back*, p. 36.

Chapter Two: Operation Enduring Freedom

18. George W. Bush, "Text: Bush Announces Strikes Against Taliban," transcript, *Washington Post*, October 7, 2001. www.washington post.com.

19. Richard W. Stewart, "Operation Enduring Freedom," US Army Center of Military History, March 17, 2006. www.history.army.mil.

20. Stewart, "Operation Enduring Freedom."

21. Stewart, "Operation Enduring Freedom."

22. Anderson, *Bush's Wars*, p. 84.

23. Quoted in Anderson, *Bush's Wars*, p. 86.

24. Stewart, "Operation Enduring Freedom."

25. Barton Gellman and Thomas E. Ricks, "U.S. Concludes Bin Laden Escaped at Tora Bora Fight," *Washington Post*, April 17, 2002. www.washingtonpost.com.

26. Quoted in Gellman and Ricks, "U.S. Concludes Bin Laden Escaped at Tora Bora Fight."

27. Stewart, "Operation Enduring Freedom."

28. Berntsen and Pezzullo, *Jawbreaker*, p. 310.

Chapter Three: The Taliban Resurgence

29. Quoted in Thomas H. Johnson, "The Taliban Insurgency and an Analysis of Shabnamah (Night Letters)," DTIC, September 2007. www.dtic.mil.

30. Quoted in Joseph J. Collins, *Understanding the War in Afghanistan*. Washington, DC: National Defense University Press, 2011, p. 74.

31. Quoted in Johnson, "The Taliban Insurgency and an Analysis of Shabnamah (Night Letters)."

32. Collins, *Understanding the War in Afghanistan*, p. 2.

33. Quoted in Paul Wiseman, "Revived Taliban Waging 'Full-Blown Insurgency,'" *USA Today*, June 6, 2006. http://usatoday30.usato day.com.

34. Wiseman, "Revived Taliban Waging 'Full-Blown Insurgency.'"
35. Quoted in Fisnik Abrashi, "3 U.S. Soldiers Killed in Afghanistan," *Washington Post*, August 12, 2006. www.washingtonpost.com.
36. Ballard, Lamm, and Wood, *From Kabul to Baghdad and Back*, p. 137.
37. Senlis Afghanistan, *An Assessment of the Hearts and Minds Campaign in Southern Afghanistan*. London: MF, 2006, p. i.
38. Senlis Afghanistan, *An Assessment of the Hearts and Minds Campaign in Southern Afghanistan*, p. ii.
39. Quoted in Satyam Khanna, "Pentagon: Taliban Growing into a 'Resilient Insurgency,'" Think Progress, June 27, 2008. http://thinkprogress.org.

Chapter Four: The Surge
40. Barack Obama, "Barack Obama's Inaugural Address," transcript, *New York Times*, January 20, 2009. www.nytimes.com.
41. Quoted in Peter Baker, "How Obama Came to Plan for 'Surge' in Afghanistan," *New York Times*, December 5, 2009. www.nytimes.com.
42. Quoted in Baker, "How Obama Came to Plan for 'Surge' in Afghanistan
43. Quoted in Anderson, *Bush's Wars*, p. 222.
44. Quoted in Anderson, *Bush's Wars*, p. 222.
45. Chris Woods and Christina Lamb, "CIA Tactics in Pakistan Include Targeting Rescuers and Funerals," Bureau of Investigative Journalism, February 4, 2012. www.thebureauinvestigates.com.
46. C.J. Chivers et al., "View Is Bleaker than Official Portrayal of War in Afghanistan," *New York Times*, July 25, 2010. www.nytimes.com.
47. Quoted in Elliot, "Biden's One-Sentence Summary of the Afghan War."
48. Quoted in Rob Taylor and Jonathon Burch, "Taliban Declares Start of Spring Offensive in Afghanistan," *Huffington Post*, April 30, 2011. www.huffingtonpost.com.
49. Quoted in Mark Landler and Helene Cooper, "Obama Will Speed Pullout from War in Afghanistan," *New York Times*, June 22, 2011. www.nytimes.com.
50. Quoted in Bill Roggio, "Mullah Omar Addresses Green-on-Blue Attacks," *Threat Matrix* (blog), August 16, 2012. www.longwarjournal.org.

Chapter Five: What Was the Impact of the War in Afghanistan?

51. John Hanrahan, "The War Without End Is a War with Hardly Any News Coverage," Nieman Watchdog, August 10, 2011. www.niemanwatchdog.org.

52. Vanessa Williamson and Erin Mulhall, "Invisible Wounds," Iraq and Afghanistan Veterans of America, January 2009. http://iava.org.

53. Costs of War, "US Veterans and Military Families," 2011. http://costsofwar.org.

54. Quoted in Gregg Zoroya, "Number of Homeless Iraq, Afghan Vets Doubles," *Army Times*, December 2102. www.armytimes.com.

55. Quoted in James Wright, "Have Americans Forgotten Afghanistan?," *Atlantic*, March 25, 2013. www.theatlantic.com.

56. Quoted in Jeremy Herb, "Study Puts Total Price Tag for Iraq, Afghanistan Wars at More than $4 Trillion," *The Hill* (blog), March 29, 2013, http://thehill.com.

57. Joseph Stiglitz and Linda Bilmes, "No US Peace Dividend After Afghanistan," *Financial Times*, January 13, 2013. www.ft.com.

58. Barack Obama, "Obama's Speech on Drone Policy," transcript, *New York Times*, May 23, 2013. www.nytimes.com.

59. Quoted in Doyle McManus, "Where's the Enemies List?," *Los Angeles Times*, June 5, 2013. www.latimes.com.

60. Quoted in Jeff Stein, "Spy Talk," *Washington Post*, March 3, 2011. http://voices.washingtonpost.com.

61. Quoted in Conor Friedersdorf, "Former State Department Official: Team Bush Knew Many at Gitmo Were Innocent," *Atlantic*, April 26 2013. www.theatlantic.com.

62. Scott Roehm, "House Debate on Closing Gitmo a Step in the Right Direction," Constitution Project, June 17, 2013. www.constitutionproject.org.

63. Quoted in Hope Reese, "Women Tell Dirty Jokes, Rely on Opium, and Other Insights from Afghanistan," *Atlantic*, May 30, 2013. www.theatlantic.com.

Important People of the War in Afghanistan

Gary Berntsen: As a CIA officer, Berntsen served as the commander of all CIA forces in eastern Afghanistan. He later wrote *Jawbreaker*, a book blaming the US military for allowing Osama bin Laden to escape from Tora Bora.

George W. Bush: Bush was only several months into his first term as president when the September 11, 2001, attacks occurred. His administration laid the foundations for the global war on terror, which continued for years after his presidency ended. Bush was commander in chief of the US armed forces during the wars in Afghanistan and Iraq during his two terms in office.

Dick Cheney: As one of the most powerful vice presidents in history, Cheney was the prime architect of the Bush administration's war on terror. Cheney made numerous public statements falsely linking Iraqi leader Saddam Hussein to the 9/11 attacks and was a strong proponent of the 2003 US invasion of Iraq.

Richard A. Clarke: Appointed National Coordinator for Security, Infrastructure Protection, and Counter-terrorism in 1998 by President Bill Clinton, Clarke retained that position in the Bush administration but was no longer given cabinet-level access. Clarke gave urgent early warnings about the al Qaeda terrorist threat before the September 11, 2001, attacks but was largely ignored.

Tommy Franks: Franks was the commander of the US Central Command overseeing the armed forces and led the attack on the Taliban during the first phase of Operation Enduring Freedom in Afghanistan.

Hamid Karzai: Karzai was named chair of the interim government of Afghanistan and was elected president of that nation in 2004, a post he held throughout the war. Karzai, who had been on the CIA payroll since the 1980s, was alleged to be in collusion with some of the country's most corrupt and abusive officials.

Osama bin Laden: Born to a wealthy Saudi Arabian family, Bin Laden was an Islamic fundamentalist who used his fortune to found al Qaeda, which conducted numerous terrorist attacks throughout the world in the 1990s. As the mastermind behind the 9/11 attacks in New York City and Washington, DC, Bin Laden was the world's most wanted terrorist until he was killed by US Navy SEALs in May 2011.

Stanley A. McChrystal: McChrystal was a US Army general who initiated the troop surge and commanded the US-led coalition forces in Afghanistan beginning in June 2009. McChrystal was forced to resign in 2010 after a magazine published disparaging remarks he had made about Obama administration officials.

Khalid Sheikh Mohammed: As a highly placed al Qaeda commander, Mohammed is known as the principal architect of 9/11. Captured by the CIA in 2003, Mohammed was sent to the Guantánamo Bay detention camp, where he was exposed to extreme interrogation techniques that included being waterboarded 183 times.

Barack Obama: Elected president of the United States in 2008, Obama initiated a 2009 troop surge in Afghanistan and stepped up drone warfare against terrorists in the Af-Pak region. Obama ended the war in Iraq in 2011 and negotiated the 2014 end to combat operations in Afghanistan.

Mullah Omar: Omar was the spiritual leader of the Taliban and the head of state in Afghanistan from 1996 to 2001. He escaped after the United States invaded Afghanistan and remains a fugitive despite a $10 million reward for information leading to his capture.

Condoleezza Rice: Rice was George W. Bush's national security adviser when the 9/11 terrorist attacks occurred. She was a major proponent of the war in Iraq and repeatedly alleged that Saddam Hussein was building a nuclear bomb, a charge that proved to be false.

Donald Rumsfeld: As defense secretary during most of the George W. Bush administration, Rumsfeld led the military planning and invasion of both Afghanistan and Iraq. In 2006 Rumsfeld was forced to resign because the wars in both nations were going badly.

For Further Research

Books

Noah Berlatsky, ed., *The War on Terror*. Farmington Hills, MI: Greenhaven, 2012.

Leanne K. Currie-McGhee, *David Petraeus*. Farmington Hills, MI: Lucent, 2011.

Deborah Ellis, *Kids of Kabul: Living Bravely Through a Never-Ending War*. Toronto: Groundwood, 2012.

Deborah Ellis, *My Name Is Parvana*. Toronto: Groundwood, 2012.

Rafal Gerszak and Dawn Hunter, *Beyond Bullets: A Photo Journal of Afghanistan*. Toronto: Annick, 2011.

Arthur Gillard, ed., *The War in Afghanistan*. Farmington Hills, MI: Greenhaven, 2013.

Lauri S. Scherer, ed., *The Taliban*. Farmington Hills, MI: Greenhaven, 2013.

Gerry Souter and Janet Souter, *War in Afghanistan and Iraq: The Daily Life of the Men and Women Serving in Afghanistan and Iraq*. London: Carlton, 2011.

Websites

Afghanistan (www.understandingwar.org/afghanistan). This site, maintained by the Institute for the Study of War, provides a comprehensive view of the Afghan war, including details on the changing security and political dynamics, the pattern of enemy activity in Af-Pak, the military operations by coalition and Afghan forces, and the political, economic, and demographic dynamics underlying the conflict.

Afghanistan War, CNN (http://topics.cnn.com/topics/afghanistan_war). In-depth reporting, articles, and videos both old and new about the Afghan war, including the politics, the Taliban, terrorism, the armed forces, and events in Pakistan.

Afghanistan War Blog, Huffington Post (www.huffingtonpost.com/news/afghanistan-war-blog). This site provides the latest news about Afghanistan, with articles about insider attacks, casualties among soldiers and civilians, the Taliban, military matters, and much more.

Costs of War (www.costsofwar.org). The Costs of War site is compiled and updated by more than thirty economists, anthropologists, lawyers, humanitarian workers, and political scientists. Together they analyze the price paid in lives and money during the wars in Afghanistan, Iraq, and Pakistan.

Iraq and Afghanistan Veterans of America (IAVA) (http://iava.org). The IAVA is the largest organization for veterans of the wars in Iraq and Afghanistan, with more than two hundred thousand veterans and supporters nationwide. In addition to offering aid and advice to veterans, the site includes a press and bloggers section with articles, statistics, and current events concerning the 2.4 million who served in uniform after 9/11.

MILblogging.com (www.milblogging.com). As of mid-2013 this site featured 3,739 blogs from military personnel, relatives, reporters, contractors, and others, with searchable databases for Afghanistan, Iraq, and other operations. Many of these blogs provide unfiltered, eyewitness accounts of battles, blunders, and even joys to be found in modern war zones.

Real Combat Life (www.realcombatlife.com). This site provides a detailed look into life in a combat zone, from exciting battle stories to the daily lives of those in harm's way. The site features photos, blogs, biographies, and other information about those fighting in Afghanistan and Iraq.

Tragedy Assistance Program for Survivors (TAPS) (www.taps.org). The human costs of the wars in Afghanistan and Iraq can be found on this website, which offers emotional support and hope to the families and friends of fallen soldiers. The site offers statistics, survivors' stories, and ways average citizens can provide help.

Index

Note: Boldface page numbers indicate illustrations.

Picture Credits

About the Author

Stuart A. Kallen is the author of more than 250 nonfiction books for children and young adults. He has written on topics ranging from the theory of relativity to the history of rock and roll. In addition, Kallen has written award-winning children's videos and television scripts. In his spare time he is a singer/songwriter/guitarist in San Diego.